New Entrepreneur's Guidebook

Leading Your Venture to Business Success

New Entrepreneur's Guidebook

Leading Your Venture to Business Success

Paul F. McClure, Ph.D.

Viva Books Private Limited
New Delhi • Mumbai • Chennai • Kolkata • Bangalore

First Indian Edition 2004

VIVA BOOKS PRIVATE LIMITED

- 4262/3 Ansari Road, Daryaganj, New Delhi 110 002
  E-mail: viva@vivagroupindia.net
- 215-216 New Apollo Estate, 2nd Floor, Mogra Lane, Andheri (E),
  Mumbai 400 069 E-mail: vivamumbai@vivagroupindia.net
- 7 Aziz Mulk, Seventh Street, Thousand Lights, Chennai 600 006
  E-mail: vivachennai@vivagroupindia.net
- B–103, Jindal Towers, 21/1A/3, Darga Road, Kolkata 700 017
  E-mail: vivakolkata@vivagroupindia.net
- 7 Sovereign Park Apts., 56-58 K. R. Road, Basavanagudi,
  Bangalore 560 004 Email: vivabangalore@vivagroupindia.net

Published by arrangement with

Crisp Publications. Inc.
1200 Hamilton Court,
Menlo Park
CA 94025
USA

ISBN 81-7649-652-9

Published by Vinod Vasishtha for Viva Books Private Limited, 4262/3 Ansari Road, Daryaganj, New Delhi 110 002 and printed at Raj Press, R-3 Inderpuri, New Delhi – 110012.

Contents

Introduction

The *New Entrepreneur's Guidebook* offers a proven framework for growing your technology-oriented business from start-up to maturity. For the first-time business builder, this book is a good substitute for experience. For the experienced manager, it is an effective team-building tool. In fact, this is the guidebook I wish I had had when I put my first company together.

Many business books that address the perennial subject, "How to start your own business" often provide helpful tips and suggestions. But, they rarely draw a map for those who have never navigated the stormy seas of building and growing a business. Most business builders are not very good mapmakers. Those who have made the journey seldom pause to draw a map. Those who do tend to focus on the start-up leg, while leaving out the middle and the end (as if would-be business builders no longer require a map once they have made it beyond safe harbor and out into deep water). Still others are sure every business is so unique that no repeatable pattern for building and growing the business can be found. They would rather sell their secrets to success case by case. In short, entrepreneurial knowledge and experience gained through trial and error, good fortune, and instinct are trapped in the realm of mystique. The real secrets of building a business all the way from start-up to maturity slip beyond the reach of most entrepreneurs.

You have to *grow with your business*. Sweat equity creates a personal bond between the founder and the company that is vital to the company's existence in its early stages. However, this same personal bond inhibits growth in the long term. You must change and grow as your company grows. Ironically, to stay in control, you must turn over large amounts of control to others. By the time your company reaches maturity, your job description will have changed completely.

You also should *never lose sight of the big picture*. Entrepreneurs steeped in technology or some other knowledge domain are naturally task-oriented. Therefore, they often lose sight of the big picture and fall into what I call the *fragmentation trap*. They think they are working on core processes critical to the life of the new company, while in reality they're just diving into a maze of fragmented tasks. They try to manage it all, but can't establish controls fast enough to keep the pieces together. In the end, everything falls apart and the business fails. Avoid the fragmented, task-centered view. Adopt a *process-centered view* from the beginning. Processes that are set up right in the first place only need to be improved with time.

This book shows you how to design and build your business from the keel up. It documents an organized view of the thought process seasoned veterans apply. Once you see how all the pieces fit together, writing your business plan becomes a matter of filling in the details of a story you already know.

I.

The Lifecycle Navigation Framework

SUCCESSFUL BUSINESSES DON'T JUST HAPPEN. They are designed and built. Veteran business builders make decisions based on the likely outcomes of present choices. They can identify the processes set in motion by a business idea. They can predict how these processes convert the natural force of their ideas into products and services with the power to win and hold customers. Experience teaches them to base their judgment on a repeatable pattern that can be understood and described. I call this pattern the *lifecycle navigation framework* because it helps you find your way from start to finish. Figure 1 shows the four basic parts of this framework.

The Prime Movers

Market creation, product development, and organizational growth are the prime movers that propel your business forward. Each prime mover develops in five natural stages as the business grows from start-up to maturity. Lifecycle

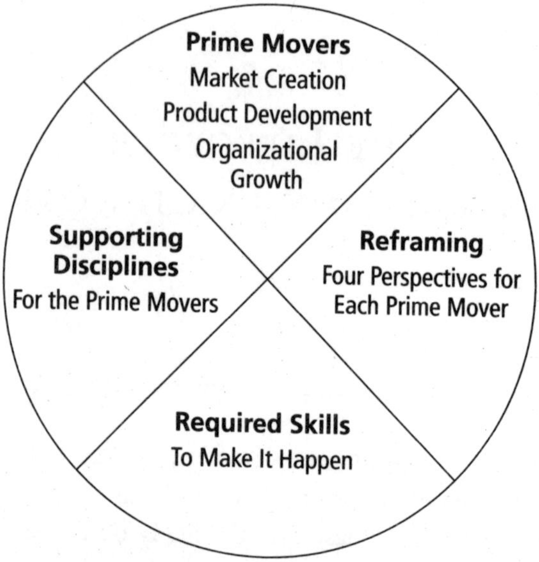

Figure 1. ***The four basic parts of the lifecycle navigation framework***

navigation exploits the predictability of these five growth stages. Identifying the growth stage your business is in provides the navigational fix you need to steer your company through the challenges that lie ahead.

The Five Stages of Market Creation

The market creation process leads to the widespread acceptance of your product or service by mainstream customers. Its five natural growth stages are:

1. Market definition
2. Technology/Domain focus

3. Product positioning
4. Market positioning
5. Company positioning

Technology enthusiasts and domain experts are the first to notice your new product offering (Stage 1). They value technology for its own sake, even before a product exists (Stage 2). A subsequent group of customers focuses its attention on the product, which must work well and deliver value to keep the customers' attention (Stage 3). Next, your customers recognize your product as a solution to a need in the mainstream marketplace (Stage 4). After customers have learned to value the ability of your company's product to fulfill an important market need, their attention turns to the company itself (Stage 5). For the firm and its products to remain in their good graces, customers must ultimately believe your company is here to stay.

The Five Stages of Product Development

The five product development stages are:

1. Product definition
2. Product design and early introduction
3. Product testing and improvement
4. Mainstream product launch
5. Lifecycle management

Product development must be a disciplined, structured process. If it is too unstructured, the creativity of product developers will cause the early product definition and product design stages to spill over into the later stages. Skipping the early product development stages is penny-wise, but pound-foolish.

The Five Stages of Organizational Growth

The five stages of organizational growth are:

1. Precommitment
2. New venture
3. Expansion
4. Professionalization
5. Maturity

The organization recreates itself each time it enters a new stage. In so doing, it gains the ability to handle an increasing number of tasks. An organization is basically a communication system. It acquires greater "bandwidth" at each new stage.

Growing a business is like raising a child. Before it can commit to life in the real world and take its breath as a new venture, the business must outgrow the embryonic stage of the business idea. The new venture's founder must feed it, change it, protect it, and get it to take its first steps in the marketplace. During the expansion stage, the organization behaves like a kid in a candy store–it grabs everything it sees. During the professionalization stage, the organization is like an adolescent, testing limits and learning rules. The mature organization takes its place in the world and starts creating wealth on a grand scale. A leader who understands how to balance management control with innovation can keep an organization in the maturity stage indefinitely. As soon as innovation stagnates, however, the organization will die a bureaucratic death.

The Power of Reframing

You have to look at most things in life from different perspectives to get the whole picture. Lifecycle navigation turns this idea into a powerful frame shifting, or *reframing,* technique: the systematic viewing of each prime mover process from its own four characteristic perspectives or frames.

A frame is a set of concepts and assumptions about reality within which people assign meaning to observed events. Reframing occurs whenever you replace one frame of reference with another. Try to view your entire business through different frames. Reframing gives you the big picture; it gives you absolute situation awareness. Reframing has to become second nature to you. It already *is* second nature to the experienced business leaders. Figure 2 shows the three prime mover processes–market creation, product development, and organizational growth. Each process is subdivided into four sections or *frames.* The following provides a closer look at each set of frames.

The Four Market Creation Frames

In each of the five growth stages the market creation process is viewed in the following four frames:

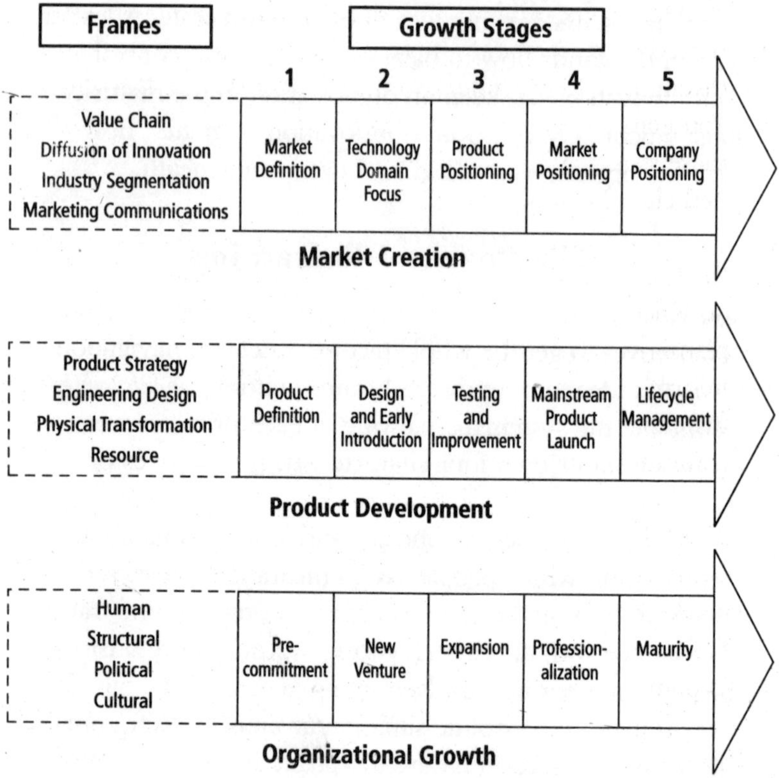

Figure 2. Reframing the three prime movers

- Value chain
- Diffusion of innovation
- Industry segmentation
- Marketing communications

The *value chain* frame breaks the company's processes down into clusters of activities that are relevant from a strategic point of view. This enables you to understand the behavior of costs and pinpoint sources of added value that distinguish your products from those of your competitors. You gain competitive advantage by being able to perform these strategically relevant process clusters better, faster, and cheaper than other firms.

The *diffusion of innovation* frame focuses attention on the time dimension. It helps you get a handle on the rate at which market potential will be realized over a future planning period after a new product is launched. This information provides critical input to your plans for raw materials acquisitions, production, staffing, marketing communications, and product support.

The *industry segmentation* frame provides a structured view of the industry in which you and your competitive rivals vie for customers. Industry segments differ markedly in the nature of customers' value chains and therefore in the type of value chain your firm must have to compete for their business.

The *marketing communications* frame views every action by your company as part of a dialog with potential customers. Communication is a closed loop process. It involves receiving as well as sending messages. The feedback loop connecting your firm to its customers is central to the operation of a market-driven company. Your communications must be flexible and responsive. Listen for the next critical message at each stage of market creation, then send the right signal to let the market know that you "got it."

The Four Product Development Frames

In each of the five growth stages the product development process is viewed in the following four frames:

- Product strategy
- Engineering design
- Physical transformation
- Resource

The *product strategy* frame views products as weapons in the overall corporate strategic arsenal. You can use it to identify product development scenarios that are likely to achieve success while minimizing risk. This frame coaxes you out of the "technology push" mentality and into the "market-pull and market-building" mindset.

The *engineering design* frame enables you to view product development in terms of the means by which input resources are transformed into a product that meets customer needs. Engineering fundamentals, manufacturability, reliability, and cost effectiveness are central to the engineering design frame.

The *physical transformation* frame provides the basis for creative brainstorming. Your design team and technical domain experts can use it to generate many off-the-wall ideas, then successively apply real-world constraints to narrow the field.

The *resource* frame first views product development as a load on the human, financial, and material resources of the organization. This resource demand load must be carried until the product starts generating revenue. You use the resource frame to profile required input, including capital equipment, engineering design talent, production system overhead, direct labor, direct materials, and general administrative overhead; and to view the trade-offs that are the basis of long-term viability.

The Four Organizational Growth Frames

In each of the five growth stages the organizational growth process is viewed in the following four frames:

- Human
- Structural
- Political
- Cultural

The *human* frame considers the individual employee's viewpoint and personality. Advocates of the human frame focus on job satisfaction, career growth, and the general well-being of the individual. The human frame also accommodates four distinct personality types. A different mix of personality types must hold sway at different stages in the life of your company.

Structure is necessary to coordinate tasks. The *structural* frame emphasizes formal roles and relationships. Organizations allocate resources and create rules to coordinate their activities. The work structure can be process-centered or task-centered. Organization charts identify who is responsible for processes or tasks. The reward system is also part of the structural frame.

The *political* frame looks at the organization from the personal power viewpoint. It places ultimate value on command and control. As Oliver Wendell Holmes observed, "The only prize much cared for by the powerful is power. The prize of the General is not a bigger tent, but command." The situation is like meteorology. The conventional systems you have established are adequate for coping with normal corporate "weather." Winning the inevitable political fight is like riding out a storm at sea. You do it when you have to, and then you fight to win.

The *cultural* frame departs from the rational. It enters the realm of myth and metaphor. It encompasses the saga of the firm's origins and rise to prominence. Leadership style emerges within the cultural frame. Behavioral norms permeate the organization, whether articulated or not. Corporate culture takes over where rules and reward systems leave off. Your business must ultimately build a viable culture to survive as a mature organization.

Supporting Disciplines for Your Growth Strategy

The lifecycle navigation map is not yet complete. Your business exists within a competitive environment. It requires either external or internal sources of financing. It must operate within the law. These are facts of life. The prime mover processes need constraints to make your growth strategy work in the real world. Do not think of competitive strategy, finance, and business law as the dynamic forces that propel your company forward. Think of them as constraints that support your business activities. I call these constraints *supporting disciplines*. Lifecycle navigation shows you how to get the working knowledge of these supporting disciplines that you need to keep from running aground.

Required Skills for the Lifecycle Navigator

For the lifecycle navigator, it takes more than a conceptual framework to run a business. It takes specific skills. In fact, so many specific skills are needed that the complete list can be intimidating. The prime mover processes that you own and the three supporting disciplines about which you are acquiring a working knowledge are all you need to command the ship. Your crew, however, needs many skills to keep the rigging intact. These needs are triggered by either the prime movers or the supporting disciplines. Lifecycle navigation shows you how to build an inventory of *required skills*. It shows you how to determine which skills you must have yourself or access right away and which ones you can develop or acquire later. Don't be intimidated. Specialized skills are for sale. If you do not have the ones you need, you can go out and get them.

II.

Deciding What Your Company Is All About

STRATEGIC VISION IS AKIN to faith–"the substance of things hoped for, the evidence of things not seen."[1] It springs from ambition and enthusiasm. Decide what your company is all about, with firm intent but flexible means. Resource limitations are challenges to be overcome, not barriers to progress.

Your business strategy should start with an over-the-horizon view of your company and its place in the world (see Figure 3). Your strategic vision should imply some distinctive competence, domain, or mission that sets your business apart from that of your competitors. You have to decide on:

- Products to be offered
- Customers to be served
- Technologies to be utilized
- Roles to be played in the industry
- Locations at which the work will be done

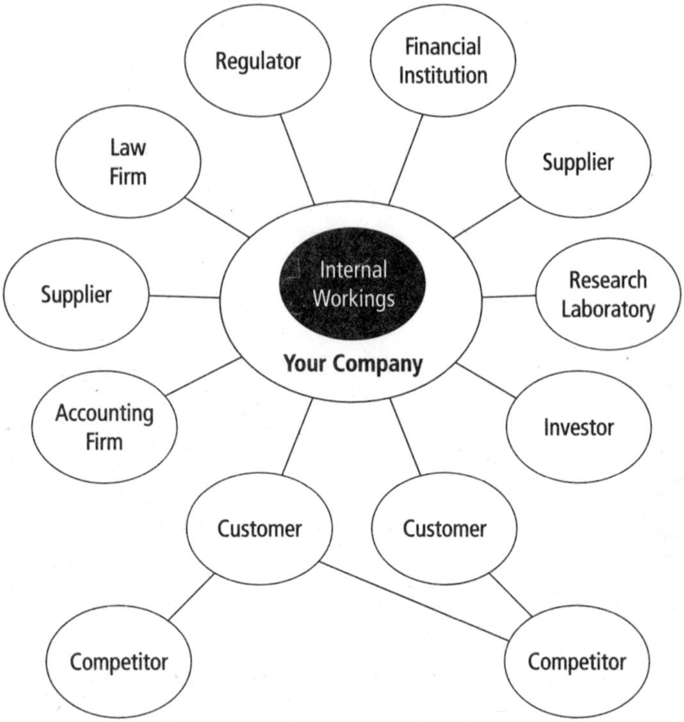

Figure 3. An over-the-horizon view of your company and its place in the world

The choices you make define your organization's points of interaction with its external environment and, by implication, the internal workings you must set up to support these interactions.

The required points of interaction with your organization's external environment set two prime movers

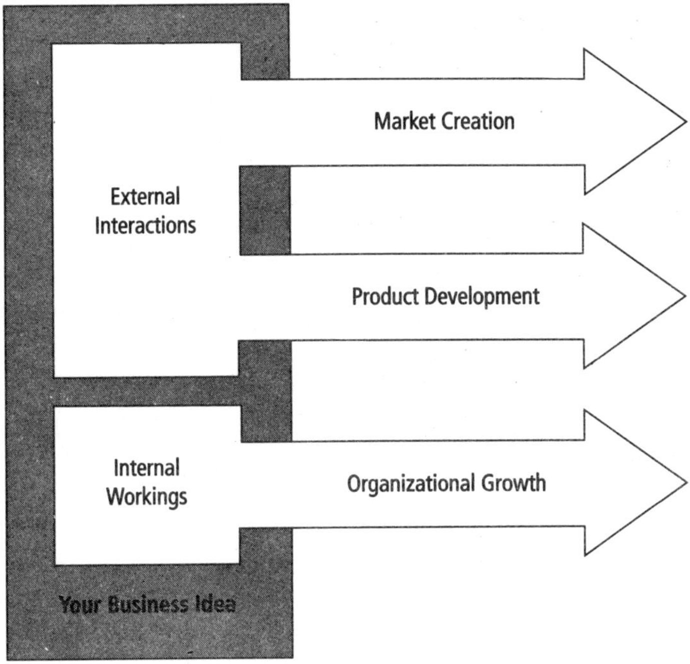

Figure 4. Your business idea sets the prime movers in motion

in motion–market creation and product development (see Figure 4). The requirement for internal workings to support interaction with the outside world sets the third prime mover in motion–organizational growth.

The first growth stage of each prime mover is the one that is involved in deciding what your company is all about. Let's use the reframing technique to examine the first stage of each prime mover, starting with market creation.

Market Creation Stage 1: Market Definition

Marketing is about gaining acceptance in the eyes of customers. Customers first accept the technology for its own sake, then in the form of a useful product. Eventually they accept the company's products as fulfilling a need in the marketplace. They ultimately come to regard the company itself as a long-term player. Market creation is not about gaining market share, although a commanding share does follow as a natural consequence. Market creation develops as your company achieves new levels of credibility in the eyes of customers.

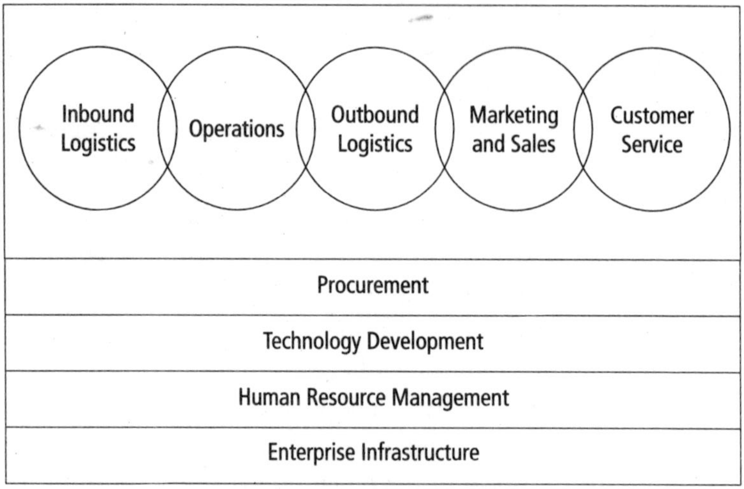

Figure 5. The value chain representation of a company (Source: Porter[2])

Value Chain Frame

The value chain frame, shown in Figure 5, represents a company as a connected group of strategically relevant activities.

Since every company fits the same mold, the activity clusters that make up its value chain can be compared with those of other companies. This provides a sound basis for comparing costs and for assessing sources of differentiation. Figure 6 looks through the eyes of the customer at two alternate worlds, one in which your company exists and one in which it does not. The customer asks, "What effect does the existence of your company, together with its suppliers and its distribution channel, have on my value chain?"

The answer to this question defines your market. Unless your product or service adds value to activity clusters in the customer's value chain, you have no market. You should be able to identify the specific places where value is added. You should be able to define the means by which your product or service generates this value in the eyes of the customer.

Diffusion of Innovation Frame

Market definition also requires an estimate of the number of customers who will eventually buy, and of the rate at which potential buyers can be converted into actual buyers. The diffusion of innovation frame provides a way to make these estimates.

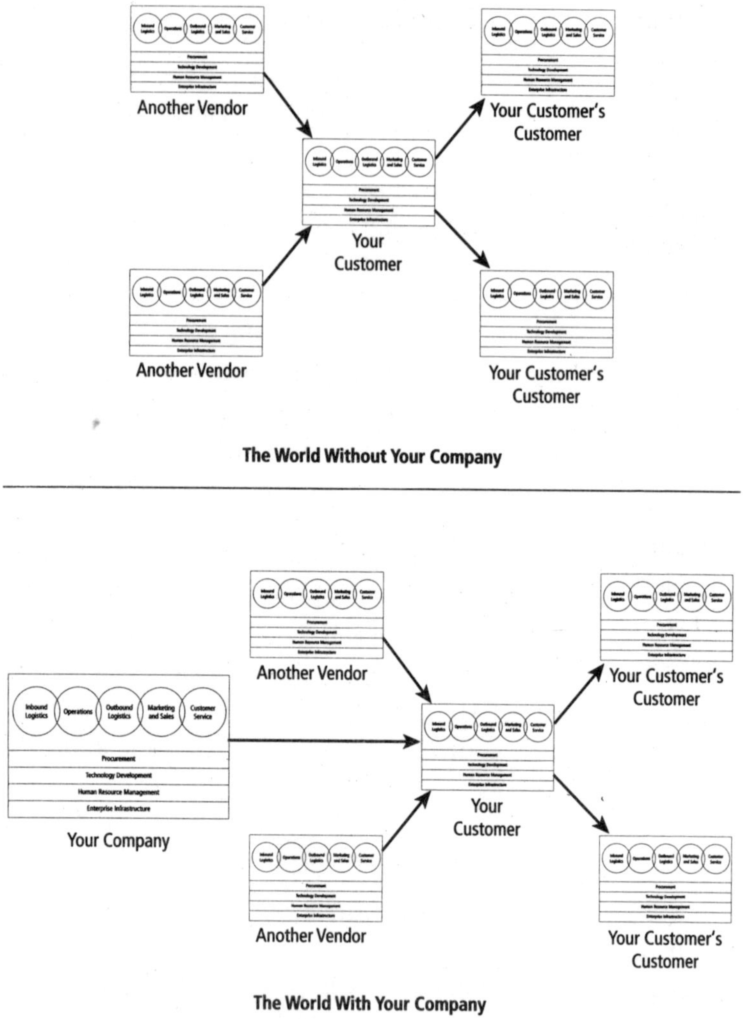

Figure 6. A customer-centered view of two alternate worlds

Start by estimating the *addressable market,* those individuals or companies with demographic (or "firmagraphic") profiles that fit what you have to offer.[3] Then estimate the *feasible market*–a subset of the addressable market that will sooner or later buy from either you or a competitor–based on subjective factors called the psychographic profile. Use the adoption curve, shown in Figure 7, to break up the market into five classic groups, based on human nature.[4]

After you decide on a reasonable time line, take the estimated feasible market size and multiply it by the respective percentages shown in Figure 7. The resulting population of actual buyers is called the *target market.* These are the customers who will buy from either you or a competitor at some time during the adoption cycle.

Next, estimate your company's share of the target market. If your product is unique, then you will create a market. Market creators start with nearly 100 percent

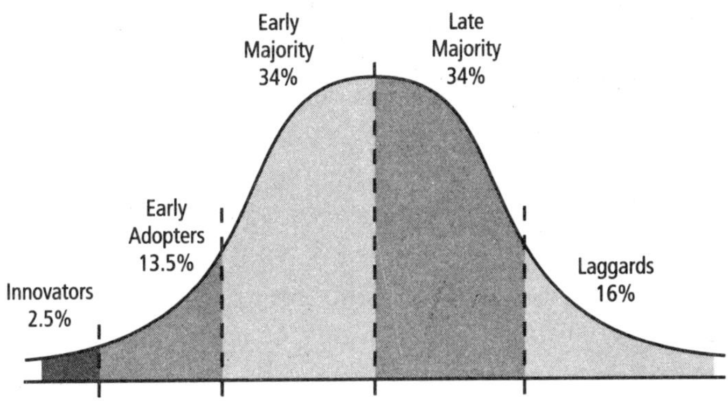

Figure 7. The adoption curve

share and typically stabilize in a range of 40 to 60 percent, depending on the intensity of the competition. If a market already exists for similar products, then you can use the fundamental theorem of market share determination to build your estimates.[5]

To project revenue, multiply your month-by-month target market estimates by the corresponding market share estimates. The result gives you *unit sales* (in units/month). Multiply your unit sales by the unit price and you have the *sales volume* (in dollars/month). Of course these numbers are only as good as your market research and your judgment.

Industry Segmentation Frame

Both customers and products differ in ways that affect the way competitive advantage is gained. Industry segmentation is a way to sort customers into groups defined by differences in the intensity and nature of competitive forces and their value chains. It includes their purchasing behavior (procurement activity) and encompasses all other primary and supporting activities in the value chain. Figure 8 shows how industry segments are defined. The columns denote buyer segmentation variables. The rows denote product segmentation variables. You segment an industry to decide what customer groups to target first and how to expand your market.

The key is to pick the right segmentation variables, based on relevant attributes of the customers, the products, and the channels that deliver products to customers. Developing a meaningful segmentation matrix is an art.

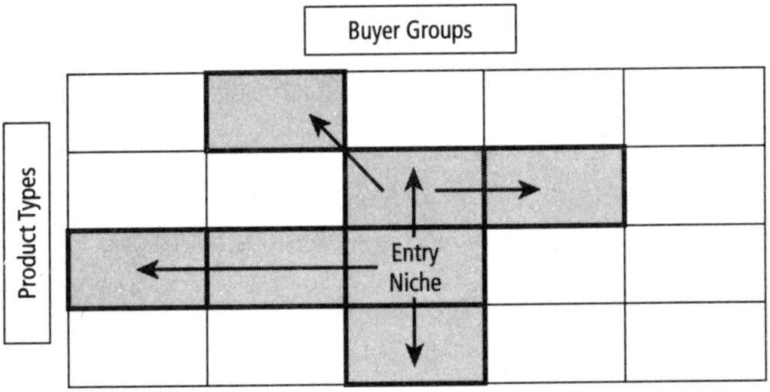

Figure 8. ***Industry segmentation, showing entry niche and expansion strategy***

In his book, *Competitive Advantage,* Michael Porter describes systematic approaches for developing a segmentation matrix.[6] You have a lot to gain from this exercise. Developing a meaningful segmentation matrix defines the field on which your battle for customer acceptance will be fought.

Marketing Communications Frame

What good is an idea, if it cannot be realized? Nailing down the following seven elements of your business idea provides what I call *reality testing:*

- A set of well-characterized customers (the targeted niche)
- An unmet need or unrealized opportunity
- A product or service to be offered for sale
- A compelling reason why customers should part with their hard-earned money

- A well-characterized set of competitors or substitutes
- A set of factors that clearly differentiate the product or service
- A good estimate of the time, talent, and treasure it will take to dominate a targeted niche

You should be listening a lot more than talking during the market definition stage. Use these seven reality-testing points to form specific questions. Then pose these questions to yourself, business colleagues, potential customers, and others. This will generate plenty of good listening opportunities. When you do get a chance to talk, you may have to keep it brief. You should be prepared to rattle off your complete business idea in the time it takes an elevator to travel three floors. It is called giving an *elevator speech.* Here is the blueprint for a script you can use to deliver your value proposition:

> [Door closes]
>
> "Hi, I'm putting a company together that will offer *product or service* to *target customers* who have *unmet need or unrealized opportunity.*"
>
> [First floor]
>
> "There's a lot of interest in this right now because *compelling reason. Target customers* will get *factors that clearly differentiate* from the company, whereas *competitors or substitutes* just provide *whatever.*"
>
> [Second floor]

"I'm raising *good estimate of treasure* and looking for *talent* to put together *an organizational vehicle* that will get us to market in *time*."

[Door opens on third floor]

Product Development Stage 1: Product Definition

Product development is about translating the voice of the customer into a tangible product. It is linked closely to market creation. Product development builds *capability,* while market creation builds *credibility*. Some products are developed to meet well-defined, expressed needs of the marketplace. In this case the voice of the customer can be heard and translated in real time. Others spring from new-to-the-world possibilities enabled by advanced technology. In this case, the voice of the customer must be anticipated.

Product Strategy Frame

Product strategy builds on the supporting discipline of competitive strategy. It springs from an analysis of your company's strengths, weaknesses, opportunities, and threats (SWOT). What is the company particularly good at? What strengths differentiate it from competitors? Where is it vulnerable? What opportunities are presented by unmet market needs or unrealized applications of new technology? What threats do competitors, industry structure, government actions, or politics pose? The answers to these questions drive product strategy.

Product strategies come in two types, active and reactive.[7] An *active* product strategy preempts future events. It achieves goals based on the power of new ideas, development or acquisition of new products, or formation of new alliances. A *reactive* strategy is defensive. It deals with outside forces as they occur. It includes imitative products, and second-but-better approaches. Both have their place, depending on the circumstances, and each should contain elements of the other.

The product definition process is highly iterative. It takes place together with market definition as shown in Figure 9.

The iteration can start in either *product space* or *market space*. It does not matter which. The important thing is that a tentative link is established connecting the two spaces.

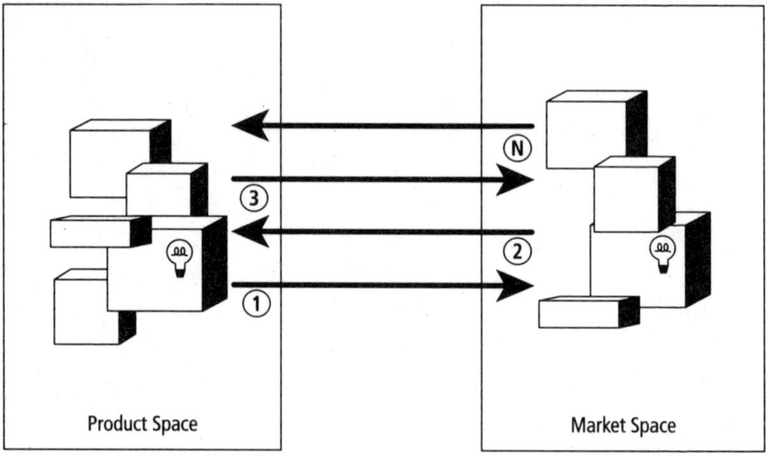

Figure 9. Product definition and market definition develop together

A dialog ensues. Product and market definition culminate when the dialog converges.

Engineering Design Frame

During the product definition stage, the voice of the customer has not yet been heard clearly enough to begin the process of translating it into a product. Instead, this frame serves as a *source* of innovative refinements to product concepts and a *reality check* on the product definition process.

Engineering design people should be present during the product strategy dialog described in the last section. Designers are good at thinking in the physical transformation frame, which is a rich source of product ideas. The discussion leader, however, should require that technical reality-check comments be withheld until as many creative out-of-the-box concepts as possible have already been generated. Reality-checking too early in the discussion stifles creativity.

Physical Transformation Frame

The physical transformation frame is the domain of the technologist. In this domain, the product appears as a system that converts matter, energy, and information into new forms that add value in the eyes of the customer. A computer, for example, converts electricity, paper, keystrokes, and mouse clicks into documents, spreadsheets, databases, and other applications stored and ready for use. All of the intermediate processes needed to achieve this conversion come to light in the physical transformation frame.

This frame can be a rich source of ideas, in addition to the technical means of their implementation. Reasoning by analogy from nature is an example. The flight of birds provided important clues for airplane wing design and flight controls. The hydrological cycle of evaporation and condensation suggested the operation of the steam engine. Vision systems and robotic devices patterned after humans and animals are also common.

Resource Frame

Resource questions come into play even at the product definition stage. Different classes of products correspond to different resource demands for development and different profit-generating potentials once in the market. The first step is to identify the main cost drivers. Start with the activities that need to occur to support the product over its life cycle: product design, testing and improvement, fabrication, direct materials and labor, marketing, sales, and lifecycle support. Assign costs based on estimates or comparisons with known cases.

Organizational Growth Stage 1: Precommitment

An organization is a group of people who join forces for a common purpose. A business organization includes the owners, a board of directors, senior executives, middle managers, and employees. Organizations are deceptive, surprising, and ambiguous if you are unaware of their natural five-stage growth pattern.

Human Frame

The business starts in the human frame, with an idea. There is usually a euphoric moment when the idea crystallizes. Those present at that moment often become the founders, investors, and key employees by default. Ideally, the founders should check and balance each other so they can do a good job of reality testing and then hang together in the new venture stage. Chance collections of people, however, are seldom the right mix. They are often similar personality types who enjoy each other's company, which is exactly the *wrong* combination. *Vive la différence!*– in business as in *l'amour.*

How do you go about adjusting the founding group without bruising egos and making enemies? It is not always possible, but you need to do it anyway. Avoid spur-of-the-moment remarks about ownership percentages and other knee-jerk comments. Keep the discussion objective and detached. Note apparent deficiencies of the founding group, but keep them to yourself until you have had time to think it through. Talk over the business idea with others you respect. Guide initial discussions to the point where a limited number of people with the right mix of viewpoints can agree on the business concept and are willing and able to bring real value to the table.

Structural Frame

The idea born in the human frame needs reality testing in the structural frame. This results in a *complete business idea* to which you can confidently ask partners, employees, and investors to commit. A complete business idea is a seven-part recipe for creating wealth. It stems from the answers to the seven reality-testing questions identified above in the marketing communications frame (pages 21–22).

Political Frame

Power politics enters into a new business in the same way that it does in forming a new government. Money brings power. A founder's ideas, however, can also create political power. Whether they do or not depends on how easily others can exploit these ideas themselves. You want those with natural access to power to be the right ones to grow the business. Unfortunately, you can't do much about this. You have to recognize the situation for what it is and take it or leave it.

More than just power politics is at work in the political frame–collaboration, for example. Power politics marginalizes the great gains achievable through mutual understanding and collaboration. "A cynic," said H. L. Mencken, "is a man who, when he smells flowers, looks around for a coffin." The cynicism and pessimism that lie at the core of power games can be self-fulfilling prophecies. If you believe the world operates this way and you act on that belief, then, for you, it probably does.

Cultural Frame

In the precommitment stage, there are no written rules. Culture alone guides behavior. However, this pre-commitment stage culture is not yet the culture of the company. The individual founders bring it with them in the form of their own ethics, values, and behavioral norms. The best you can do is insist on honesty, respect, and hard work right from the start. Doing what you say you will do is a hard thing when everyone is subject to conflicts and competing priorities. It is therefore a great character test. Make reliability a behavioral norm. Later, as the company grows, the values and practices of the founders will merge into the behavioral norms of the company. This is a long-term process. It will not be complete until the maturity stage, years later.

First Lifecycle Transitions

The three prime movers–market creation, product development, and organizational growth–develop together, as shown in Figure 10. Market creation and product development converge to a *need/solution pair.* At the same time, the organization's founders and prospective investors are building up enough confidence to make firm commitments.

The first lifecycle transitions are now at hand. You must navigate *all three* transitions successfully before going on to build a viable company. Skipping any one of these three transitions creates a "birth defect" that will probably prove fatal to your business later on. The lifecycle transitions generally (but not always) occur at about the same time. For example, the market and product could be defined quickly, but founders or investors might take a long time to commit. Conversely, real commitment

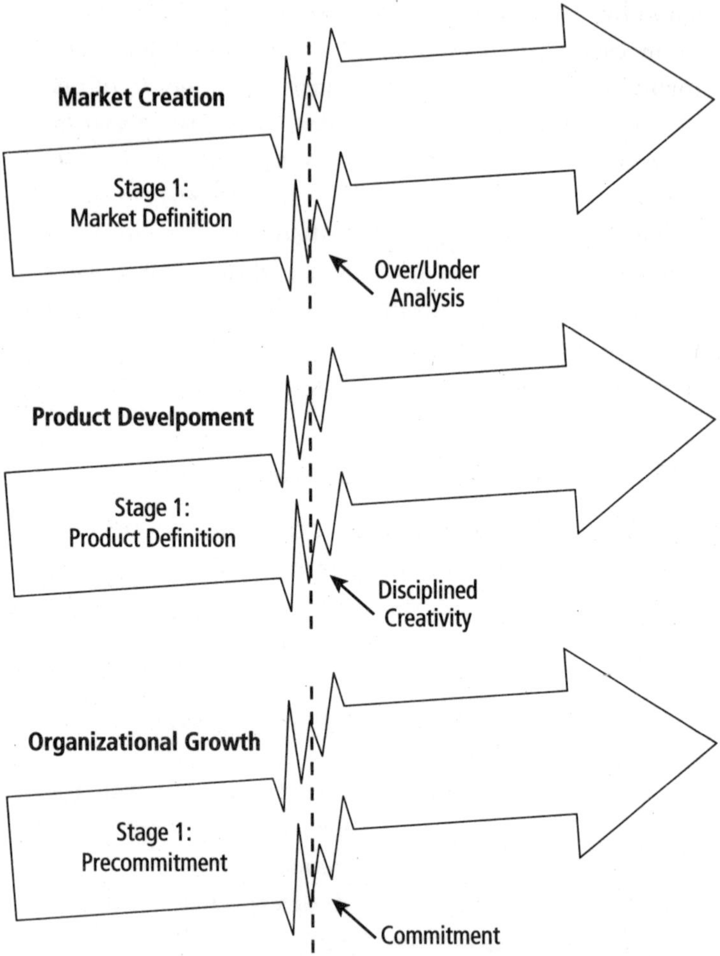

Figure 10. The three prime movers approach their first lifecycle transitions

could be established early based on people who already know each other well and want to work together, but it might take longer to define a viable market and product.

Do not let product definition and market definition get too far out of step. Entrepreneurs, whose main experience is technology-based, often find it much easier to define the product than to define the market. However, moving forward without reality testing and a reasonable market size estimate can create wildly optimistic expectations. Many starry-eyed friends have become dejected adversaries when such hopes were dashed.

Let's take a closer look at the first three lifecycle transitions.

The Crisis of Overanalysis or Underanalysis

Many entrepreneurs make one of two common mistakes in transitioning from market definition to the next stage of market creation. First, there is *overanalysis,* otherwise known as "analysis paralysis." You can never take out all the risk. Devote a reasonable amount of effort to analyzing your market. Then try and learn. This is particularly true of new-to-the-world products for which no market yet exists. In this case, you are a market creator. You will make history for others to analyze. The other extreme, *underanalysis,* is equally deadly. Leaping before looking invites defeat. It loses the very first round of the credibility-building game.

The Crisis of Disciplined Creativity

Discipline and creativity may seem poles apart. Yet they must join forces to propel product development to the next stage. A structured product development process will help you get through this and subsequent transitions. First, a product approval team should be formed to manage the product development pipeline. This team includes the CEO plus the heads of marketing, manufacturing, engineering, and finance. These positions may not all be filled at an early stage. If necessary, complete your product approval team with outside experts. The product approval team directs and manages product development efforts so that business goals and strategies are achieved. It also conducts phase reviews and makes phase review decisions. A core team presents issues and results for phase review. This core team is a small cross-functional team, appointed by the product approval team and headed up by a core team leader. It works to develop and introduce products or enhancements. The core team makes brief, comprehensive phase review presentations of business and technical issues to the product approval team, which then decides to fund the next phase, redirect work, or terminate the project. The product approval team conducts five phase reviews:

1. **Idea stage review.** Occurs at the end of the product definition stage. Deliverables include preliminary business assessment, preliminary technology assessment, and preliminary product development plan.

2. **System concept review.** Occurs during the product design and early introduction stage. Deliverables include system architecture, high-level design, technology assessment, product/system specifications, project plan, and a preliminary plan for testing and documentation.

3. **Detailed design review.** Occurs at the end of the product design and early introduction stage. Deliverables include prototype alpha (in-house) development, prototype beta (customer's site) development, test plan, documentation plan, preliminary vendor specifications and sourcing, preliminary service and support development, and preliminary product launch plan.

4. **Test and readiness review.** Occurs during the test and evaluation stage. Deliverables include manufacturing verification, internal tests, market probes, final vendor specifications and sourcing, service and support plan, and final market launch plan (i.e., the plan for crossing the chasm).

5. **Implementation review.** Occurs just prior to the product launch. Deliverables include product release, product launch, and review of lessons learned.

The Crisis of Commitment

The business idea dies if no one makes a real commitment. A real commitment means quitting a regular job to take charge of running the business full-time. It means putting up hard-earned cash equivalent to the price of a new house or a new car. It means committing to build a working prototype by hand in a garage by a certain date and then making it happen no matter what. It does not mean finding some hireling to go out and run the business, while the principals keep their regular jobs, collect their paychecks, and talk it up on the golf course.

The *reason* for making the commitment can be just as important as the commitment itself. Are those putting up time and treasure only in it for a return on investment? If so, that is not enough motivation this early in the game. There is a good reason why purely money-oriented people seldom start companies: too much risk is involved. They shouldn't. A good, red-blooded entrepreneur certainly has no problem with return on investment. But the real driver is the founder's commitment to the idea itself–the burning vision of the product being used and appreciated. Return on investment may never materialize. If it does not, the business will grind to a halt somewhere down the road. The promise of a financial return alone cannot make the deal happen. Right now, to get it started, you have to believe in the *dream.*

Let me rephrase that. *You* have to believe in the dream. If you do not believe in it, nobody will. Certainly your potential customers will not believe in it, not yet. It is *your* vision. As the entrepreneur, you project both the need *and* the product that meets the need. This whole new need/solution pair is being readied for an unsuspecting world. I do not mean to denigrate the tried-and-true maxim, "find a need and fill it." That will work. However, by the time you have spotted an obvious need, other enterprising souls will have spotted it, too. You could be sharing the winner's circle with a good-sized herd. The business ideas with the most *reach* are always flavored with a dash of prophecy. They get out ahead of the customer, but not too far ahead. They give customers what they will soon figure out they need, not necessarily what they already know they need.

III.

Growing Your Business

Businesses, like people, grow up in different ways. Like people, businesses typically also pass through the same sequence of predictable growth stages. Figure 11 depicts the growth of your business as the unfolding of the stages of each prime mover process.

The signposts mark lifecycle transitions. The elevation gains convey the notion of the growing scope and intensity of activity. The last set of transitions is the most difficult of all to survive. These transitions mark the boundary between an entrepreneurial company in its early stages and a professionally managed firm that can hold its own in a mainstream market.

Market creation and product development continue to develop in step with one another. Neither should outpace the other by even one growth stage. The technology/domain focus stage of market creation, for example, should be going on while product development is in the product design and early introduction stage. The product positioning stage of market creation and the testing and improvement stage of product development should also occur simultaneously.

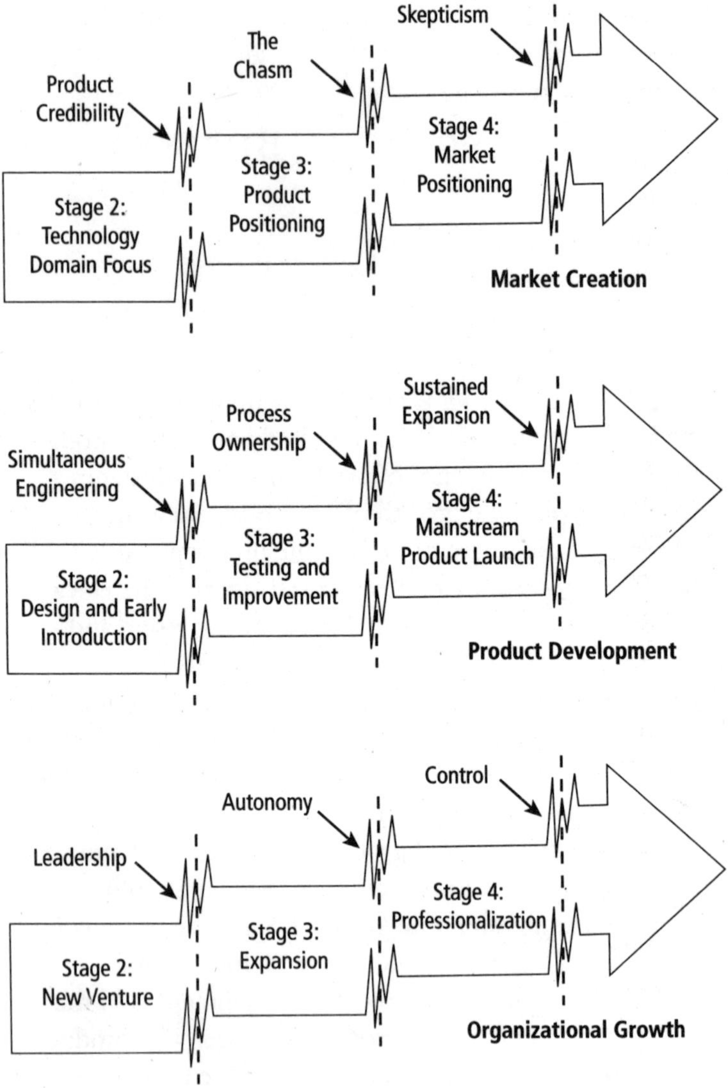

Figure 11. The growth of your business

Organizational growth, however, should move at a faster pace. There are two reasons. First, the organization must grow rapidly enough to carry the explosive information-handling load produced by market creation and product development activities. This information-handling requirement alone usually requires you to have your organization reach the professionalization or maturity stage (Stages 4 and 5 of the organizational growth process) by the time market creation reaches the product positioning stage (Stage 3 of the market creation process).

The second reason has to do with discipline. It takes a lot of discipline to cross the transitional chasm between Stages 3 and 4 in the market creation process and secure a position in the mainstream market. This requires at least an organization that has reached the professionalization stage *before* crossing that chasm. The odds of success are even greater if the organization has reached its maturity stage before crossing that chasm. It is like requiring a teenager to make it *all the way* through adolescence and, if possible, well into young adulthood before taking on the full burden of adult responsibility.

The Next Three Market Creation Stages

This section describes Stages 2, 3, and 4 of the market creation process. These stages comprise the tough-to-execute middle of the market-building journey. They will make or break your company's relationship with its customers. In Stage 2, you win over the innovators, who are the gatekeepers to the marketplace, by demonstrating command of the technology they care about. Then comes Stage 3, product positioning. Here, you win over visionaries with the resources to transform your raw capability into a product that solves a challenging problem. Stage 4, market positioning, happens when your company crosses the chasm and secures its beachhead in the mainstream market.

Market Creation
Stage 2: Technology/Domain Focus

Innovators are gatekeepers to the marketplace. Some live in the advanced technology groups of big companies, empowered to monitor the leading edge. Others are self-appointed wizards in small companies to whom others look for opinions about the latest and greatest new products. You must win them over to enter the market.

Value Chain Frame. Innovators appreciate technology for its own sake. They want the truth, not marketing hype. They want direct access to the best technologists in your own company, a desire you must handle with care. You need their confidence and feedback, but you cannot let them carry your problems and plans to competitors. Bring some of these innovators in as consultants, under secrecy agreement. Get the feedback you need in a controlled environment as quickly as possible.

Innovators are cheap. They think technology ought to be free or sold at no more than cost. If you are asking innovators to pay for the product out of their own pockets, it has to be cheap. So eliminate price as a sales barrier.

This is not the stage of market creation where your main focus is wealth generation. That comes later.

Diffusion of Innovation Frame. Innovation diffuses through the market like fluid through porous rock. It seeks the path of least resistance. Innovators are easy to reach. Just bait their watering holes. Show up at technology conferences and professional society meetings. Use computer bulletin boards and Web sites. Place ads in the trade publications they read. Use cheap little ads with a technology hook. Include a response card or a toll-free number. Offer free demonstrations.

Industry Segmentation Frame. Your market definition exercise has pinpointed groups of customers with buying patterns and value chains that fit what your product offers. These are all potential candidates for market entry. Pick your first target segment carefully. Markets, like people, do not forget first impressions. The best industry segment to enter is one whose members are well aware of themselves as a group. They intercommunicate. They listen to and believe word-of-mouth testimonials. They reference each other when making buying decisions. Look for a segment that is not too large. The pond should be just small enough that your company is noticed as a fish that is big enough to talk about.

Marketing Communications Frame. Marketing communications take on broader scope and intensity once you start selling products. Effective communication is a two-way street. Sender and receiver must both comprehend the message. Your message must be loud and clear enough to be heard above all the other messages competing for the customer's attention.

What others say about your product is always many times more credible than what you say yourself. Seek out the expert industry watchers who are frequently quoted in articles written for your industry's trade publications and newsletters. Let them in on your technology/domain focus. Share with them how you intend to meet the needs of the targeted segment. Provide demonstrations and press packages. Then refer trade publication editors, free-lance writers, and newsletter publishers to these experts. Monitor feedback. Adapt and move on. Never forget that the position you create in the market exists in the minds of customers, not in your laboratory or marketing department.

Transition: The Crisis of Product Credibility. You have won the hearts of technologists. Their zeal must now be transformed into product credibility. The transition from the technology/domain focus stage to the product positioning stage is a natural one. It requires harnessing your technology to make someone's dream come true. Technology alone is not enough to reach the next credibility plateau. It must be transformed into a *killer application,* one that a performance-oriented visionary will adopt on a pilot project basis. You enter the transition zone when you start to zero in on that killer application.

Market Creation
Stage 3: Product Positioning

Product positioning happens when visionaries with the resources to back up their dreams grab hold of your new technology and fall head over heels in love with it. Though technophiles at heart, these visionaries are true early adopters of leading-edge products, not mere technology enthusiasts. Their careers are booming. Many are already senior managers or executives. They are passionate about changing the way business is done in their industry.

Value Chain Frame. You must gain the confidence of one or more such visionaries to get your product *positioned.* They need weapons to make their mark. They will take your raw technology into their camp and commit the resources to fashion it into a product that serves as a strategic weapon. Visionaries demand blockbuster performance. They want quantum leaps. Cutting-edge technology is the means to this end, not the end itself.

Visionaries know they are living on the edge. They are willing to accept high risks and generally are not price-sensitive. They are therefore ideal financiers of your product development effort. Be careful when playing this game. Visionaries are hard to please. Their dreams expand in waves, knowing no bounds. You will be asked to invent whatever they discover to be missing.

You probably will formalize some of these relationships as beta programs. You must please these customers, and you need their money. However, do not forget that you also have a dream, which leads in another direction. To realize *your* dream, you must extract a core product from the visionary's project, one you can resell many times over to a broader market. To make the balancing act work, break the project into achievable stages. Set clear milestones. Productize the result of each milestone *in addition* to delivering the performance your customer demands. Define a clear ending point for the project. You must come out of this experience with (1) a happy visionary who is willing to serve as a customer reference and (2) a core product that can serve a broader market.

Diffusion of Innovation Frame. How do you get visionaries to bite? You cannot just bait their watering holes, like you did to attract technologists. Visionaries have no well-defined watering holes. Instead, you get the diffusion of innovation process to attract them for you. Visionaries talk to technologists. They seek them out and pump them for insights about the leading edge. If you have seeded your first target segment with enough enthusiastic technologists, sooner or later one of them will take your message to the right visionary. This will happen sooner, not later, if you have picked a target segment that is small enough for the diffusion process to work efficiently. The smaller the target niche, the higher the concentration of technologists and the shorter the lines of communication with the visionaries they talk to.

Industry Segmentation Frame. A systematic approach to industry segmentation will help in positioning your product. Start with a segmentation matrix. The columns are customer-related attributes (buyer type, geography, procurement behavior, nature of the buyer's production system–all the elements of the buyer's own value chain). The rows are product-related attributes (size, voltage, complexity, speed, accuracy, price–the features and functions that distinguish the product). Your next challenge is to reduce the number of segmentation variables to a manageable number. Eliminate variables that have no significant effect on competitive advantage or industry structure. Then look for variables that always go together. Build a new matrix with these clustered variables. Then examine each segment. Redefine your clusters to eliminate combinations of attributes that do not go together in the real world. You may have to try several schemes before you find one that represents reality. Test your matrix by positioning known competitors within the segments. If you find a natural fit, you probably have a useful tool.

Marketing Communications Frame. Every action your company takes shows up in the marketing communications frame as part of a continuous dialog with the marketplace. Many of the issues that matter to customers are subjective. Some are highly symbolic. Do not dismiss them as irrational. Listen and learn. Camps of devotees who champion this or that platform, architecture, or operating system invariably form. You will probably have to identify with one of these camps and win it over. Affiliations, customer lists, styles, and symbols are all parts of the marketing communications process.

Provide samples and demonstrations to industry watchers and commentators. Ask for critiques in return for an early look. Build a similar dialog with key suppliers. Share your present and future needs for materials, parts, and services. Ask for suppliers' advice. Talk about quality, traceability, and component selection. Open a dialog with direct salespeople, dealers, distributors, and retailers. What sells? What doesn't? What channel works best for what you have? How much support will be required? What kind of support will be required? What should you charge for it? These people already work with the same customers you will be working with. Listen to what they have to say.

Transition: The Crisis of the Chasm. The game is about to change radically. A great gulf, known as the *chasm,*[8] separates product positioning from market positioning. The transition spanning this gulf is more daunting than all the other marketing transitions combined. Approach it with care, for it is unforgiving. The last words of many a dying entrepreneurial dream have been uttered in the depths of the chasm. The reward for a successful crossing is a secure beachhead in the pragmatic mainstream market.

Market Creation
Stage 4: Market Positioning

Who are these pragmatic mainstream buyers, the early majority and late majority, who make up two-thirds of the market? What do they really value? They manage programs and run overhead functions in medium-to-large companies, nonprofits, and government agencies. They command respect without making a lot of noise. They like bundled products that provide a complete solution. They like predictable, measurable gains. Risk, for them, means waste, not opportunity. Only the demand for higher productivity has pushed them forward in the adoption cycle.

Value Chain Frame. Pragmatists care a lot about the company they are buying from. They want it to be there tomorrow, so they do not have to go to the trouble of qualifying a new vendor. They care about quality and service. They want a single point of contact to call when something needs fixing or adjusting. They like the buyer leverage that competition provides. It keeps a lid on costs and offers alternatives to any vendors who disappoint them. They also like the leverage they get by buying from the market leader. The *aftermarket* that comes with the leader is a real bonus. It provides a bigger choice of support services, compatible interfaces, and products that plug into these interfaces. Pragmatists are willing to pay for premium quality, but they still want the best deal they can get. Their price sensitivity will drive down prices, but productivity and volume will improve profitability.

Then there are the laggards, the last sixth of the market to buy. Their value proposition is mainly negative. They are skeptics who can block a purchase, but seldom initiate one. The force of the diffusion process eventually will bring them into the fold, so do not worry about it. The laggards can even do you a lot of good. Listen to their skeptical remarks carefully. They will be the first to expose the remaining cracks in the armor of what you thought was your whole product offering.

Diffusion of Innovation Frame. You have to restart the diffusion process from a beachhead in the mainstream market. References from the visionaries you satisfied in the product positioning stage are not enough. Most pragmatists want references from other pragmatists. Your first pragmatist customer is therefore the most important customer you will ever have.

The pragmatists will resist your intrusion. You must win in the face of suspicion and skepticism. Package a total solution for your targeted mainstream customer. When you are done, this package will look like a collection of services surrounding a core product. Increase your chances by targeting emerging or expanding mainstream markets. These will contain more good prospects and therefore better the odds of getting the first one to bite. There will also be fewer existing products with which to compete.

As with any invasion, the supporting infrastructure must be in place before the command is given to attack. Production facilities and distribution channels must be ready to handle the initial mainstream market demand and able to expand as it grows. Marketing communications materials must be designed and ready. The sales force must be trained. Working capital must be adequate to bankroll selling activities and finance receivables.

Pragmatists are loyal after they are won over. This works to your advantage because they make great references for selling to other pragmatists. Get a mainstream niche to standardize on your new total solution and you are off and running. Once reignited, the diffusion process will carry your business forward with more breadth and power than you have ever experienced. This is the mainstream market *pull* you are looking for.

Industry Segmentation Frame. Picking the right target segment for your entry into the mainstream market is a little like the game of billiards. You not only want to drop the ball in the right pocket, you want to set up your next shot. Once positioned in the mainstream market, you will want to "run the table." In a market creation context, this means running along either a row or a column of your industry segmentation matrix, not diagonally. Why? Because you are looking for maximum leverage. Staying with a particular row means you are leveraging the same core product across a range of buyer types. Staying with a particular column leverages your relationship with a given type of buyer, opening the door to selling these same customers different products. Eventually, you will migrate diagonally, but that takes more energy. It is better to build momentum first.

Pick your channel to help create demand. Some channels are better at creating demand; others are better at fulfilling demand after it has already been created. A direct sales force is the best at creating demand. Partnering with other vendors who agree to customize, service, or support your product can work well. Getting your solution bundled with packages offered by system integrators also helps. Avoid retail, value-added resellers, distributors, and original equipment manufacturers as primary channels until you are more established. They are better at filling orders than creating demand.

Marketing Communications Frame. The words and images your marketing people use are only part of the picture. Every act associated with your company is part of its *voice*. The market *listens* to the soundness of your whole-product solution. It hears of performance achieved here and cost saved there. It repeats stories about the timeliness and effectiveness of your customer service and support. It takes note of your ties to the known infrastructure. The credibility of your new solution to the market's problems is on trial as never before.

Competitors already serving the targeted industry segment will react instantly to your intrusion. They were willing to let you experiment with visionary projects, but now you are a real threat. Expect FUD (fear, uncertainty, and doubt) attacks aimed directly at your weakest point–credibility with mainstream customers. Your whole-product armor must be strong enough to withstand these FUD attacks. Return fire by positioning your product as the proven productivity leader within the target segment.

Defining the competition is a major market positioning theme. Pragmatic customers need a frame of reference to make comparisons. You gain the upper hand when you provide that frame for them. Any battle is already half-won if you define the terms on which it is fought. Your message must set the criteria for victory. It must paint a credible picture of your competition as well as your own product offering.

Transition: The Crisis of Skepticism. Your whole-product solution has earned the respect of pragmatists within the beachhead segment of the industry–a major achievement. Now a new battle lies ahead, the fight for *corporate* credibility in the eyes of the mainstream marketplace.

Your elevator speech needs a new script. It picks up on the theme of your growing installed base. Profitability, plant expansions, and stock placements work their way into the message. The whole array of customer support infrastructure is on display, including standard interfaces and complementary products and services offered by affiliates and aftermarket vendors.

Follow-up products emerge from your design and production activities. New segments are targeted, attacked, and won over. The marketplace watches. It concludes that your company itself is a force to be reckoned with. Your company is here to stay.

The Next Three Product Development Stages

This section describes Stages 2, 3, and 4 of the product development process. An early version of the product introduced to innovators and early adopters typically is revised several times. This process of perfecting the product starts with Stage 2, product design and early introduction. Additional risk is taken out and additional benefit is built in during Stage 3, testing and improvement. Product development enters Stage 4, mainstream product launch, when the entire product package is ready for use in the mainstream market.

Product Development
Stage 2:
Product Design and Early Introduction

The product design and early introduction stage begins with the target customers identified in the product definition stage, stage 1.

Product Strategy Frame. Use additional information about customers and the solution to form a core benefit proposition,[9] which states the unique benefits the product provides and tells what makes it superior to competing products. A core benefit proposition for a technology product might note speed, power, memory, and ease of use, and claim superior openness of its architecture. The issue is how to deliver the core benefit proposition in a tangible form. Product strategy now reduces to tactics. The structured product development process described earlier (pages 32–33) lays down the rules for this tactical engagement. Two of the five phase reviews take place during the product design and early introduction stage: the system concept review (Phase 2) and the detailed product design review (Phase 3). Following the structured process assures that producibility, reliability, maintainability, and supportability issues will be anticipated right up front in addition to cost. Quality must be designed in at every step. That way, mistakes do not have to be inspected out over the life of the product.

Engineering Design Frame. The product development team takes three major steps during the product design and early introduction stage that are best viewed in the engineering design frame: requirements definition, concept design, and detailed product design.

Requirements definition identifies overall end-user needs and converts these into initial performance, cost, producibility, quality, and reliability objectives the product must meet.

Concept design trades off different product design approaches and technologies in search of the best method for delivering the core benefit proposition. Analyses, mathematical modeling, simulation, and cost estimates are performed. Concept product design produces guidelines, product design requirements, program plans, and other documentation. The Phase 2 review is conducted at this point.

Detailed design creates a prototype that meets or exceeds requirements. Lessons learned from further analysis are used to improve the product design. Laboratory models may be built for testing and evaluation. The Phase 3 review is conducted upon completion of detailed product design.

Physical Transformation Frame. A whole sequence of "whats" is converted into "hows" during the product design and early introduction stage. This important sequence appears most clearly in the physical transformation frame. Quality function deployment[10] is one formalized method to describe this process.

Resource Frame. Every event just viewed in the physical transformation frame appears as a cost driver in the resource frame. It takes talented people, design tools, laboratory space, equipment, and overhead resources to accomplish these tasks. Nothing has been sold yet, so all of the resources identified occur as loads or demands on the enterprise.

Time is an important resource, too. Can the company bring the product to market within the window of opportunity? This depends largely on how well the product design and early introduction stage is executed; that is, how quickly the voice of the customer can be embodied in a product and offered to the customer in tangible form.

Transition: The Crisis of Simultaneous Engineering. The product design and early introduction stage is a complex, highly interactive part of the product development process. Yet its goal is simple: hear the voice of the customer and translate it into a product. The talents and energies of marketing, engineering, and production people, plus financial people and senior management, must all converge to achieve this goal. This is far easier said than done. Simultaneous consideration of many design issues is required. Changes in any one domain may strongly affect all the rest.

The key is to always keep the core benefit proposition in front of the design team. One company reportedly keeps a life-sized dummy around with a sign on its chest labeled "The Customer." "The Customer" is highly visible at every design discussion.

Product Development
Stage 3: Testing and Improvement

The testing and improvement stage provides your last chance to assure seaworthiness before launching out into the deep water of the mainstream market. Viewing your whole product offering from all four product development frames reveals ways to take out risk and increase performance. The goal is to reach a "decision frontier"[11] at which you strike an appropriate risk-performance balance before executing your mainstream product launch.

Product Strategy Frame. A good design process takes much of the risk out of the product and builds in much of its ability to deliver the core benefit proposition. But neither objective is attained the first time through. Additional risk must be removed and additional benefit must be added before the company decides to launch the product. Both efforts cost money, so a three-way trade-off arises: benefit versus risk versus cost. The goal is to reach a sound product launch decision at minimum cost. Designers do a lot of iterating between the product strategy frame and the resource frame to get the right fit.

Engineering Design Frame. New problems come to light when the product is tested for the first time with all parts in place. These are typically systems problems. Interfaces do not work as planned. Environmental conditions affect the product in ways that were not foreseen. Manufacturability and reliability problems surface.

These problems must be resolved by testing and improvement before product launch and full-scale production. The core benefit proposition should always be tested on as small a scale as possible before committing to larger-scale production. The Phase 4 review (test and readiness) occurs when the core team decides that enough testing and improvement has been done.

Even more extensive customer testing is required when a whole-product package is readied for mainstream market entry. This includes test marketing to produce the best possible sales projections and pricing information. Selling tactics are also tested. For example, sales to panels of firms exposed to alternate sales tactics can be analyzed. Industrial product testing is more complex because of multiple participants in the buying decision and infrequent purchases. The first few encounters with mainstream prospects should therefore be monitored carefully. The Phase 5 review (implementation) occurs just before product launch.

Resource Frame. Many product development costs have already been incurred. However, major costs still lie ahead and more data are now available than ever before. The testing and improvement stage therefore provides the last and best opportunity to estimate production costs and assess potential returns. A chasm crossing is so resource-intensive that it is often a life-of-the-company decision. The principal shareholders are likely to be involved. New equity or debt capitalization is usually required for this specific purpose.

It is important to rework the risk versus benefit analysis in detail. The adjusted present value method[12] is useful for valuing operations, or assets-in-place. Opportunities (such as potential investments) are best valued using option-pricing methods.[13] Ownership claims (such as participation in joint ventures, partnerships, or strategic alliances) can be valued by estimating cash flows to equity.[14] A spreadsheet model can be run in Monte Carlo fashion to get a better handle on risks when assumptions are highly uncertain. Such formal valuation methods help depoliticize decision making. In the final analysis, however, intuition and common sense must weigh heavily in trading risk versus benefit.

Physical Transformation Frame. During the testing and improvement stage, the focus of the physical transformation frame shifts from creating the product to verifying that the product delivers the core benefit proposition as intended. The required disciplines include developmental testing, process engineering, software development, failure analysis, design-to-cost, producibility, manufacturing prototypes, environmental stress screening, configuration management, and customer testing.

Transition: The Crisis of Process Ownership. If things have been done right, the marketing and production people have had a hand in product development from the beginning, but the product development process itself has been "owned" by design engineers. That must now change. Ownership of product development must now be handed over to the marketing people. Why? Because the design problem has changed from a core-product design problem to a whole-product design problem. The whole-product (the core product plus added hardware and software, standards, installation procedures, documentation, interfaces, cabling, training, support, and third-party affiliations) must continue to be designed, tested, and improved in market space, not technology space. Technology continues to play a key role, but the tools it brings to the table no longer address the central issues.

This is a difficult parting of the ways. Creators of the core product often resent it deeply. They feel they are being forced to "give up their baby." But the transition must occur if the "baby" is to grow up and enter the mainstream marketplace.

Product Development
Stage 4: Mainstream Product Launch

The mainstream product launch stage is about entering a mainstream market for the first time. Do not confuse it with the first sale of an early-market product to an innovator or even the first sale of a pilot project to a visionary customer. Mainstream product launch means whole-product launch. It is the first time you intend to get pragmatic mainstream buyers to accept your whole-product solution as a viable proposition.

Product Strategy Frame. A mainstream product launch must be planned and executed like clockwork. Leave as little as possible to chance. Your goal is not to experiment with the mainstream market. It is to overcome resistance in the target niche and position yourself in the mainstream market–the very first time you try.

Once the decision to launch is made (Phase 5 review), the organization must focus all its resources on carrying out the plan. The strategy is already in place. Management's main role is to monitor the launch and take prompt action to exploit new opportunity, and to take corrective action if things start to go badly.

Engineering Design Frame. Ideally, nothing at all will show up in the engineering design frame during product launch. Nevertheless, the engineering design team should stand by in case of an emergency. What would happen, for example, if the retaining straps the packaging vendor is supposed to provide do not arrive and there is no time to order more? Your own people had better be able to invent a solution and get it working on the spot.

Critical path analysis can help. Plotting out the product launch in program evaluation and review technique (PERT) format can help spot the main schedule risks and prepare for contingencies in advance.

Physical Transformation Frame. Production and logistics dominate the physical transformation frame during a product launch. The more flexible the production system, the better. A short production cycle time enables you to ramp up or down as initial sales results come in. This way, you avoid either starving your finished goods inventory or piling up excess inventory.

On-time delivery of all parts of the whole-product solution is critical. Everything must work right out of the box. Installation services, if required, must go without a hitch. Coordination and timing are everything. These issues are especially critical if competitors are also aggressively targeting the same niche.

Resource Frame. By the time you launch your product, most of the production costs have already been designed in. Now the resource-balancing act has more to do with balancing supply and demand as sales ramp up. You want your finished goods inventory large enough to eliminate stockouts at all points of sale, but not so large that you risk excessive inventory cost. A good model of your supply, production, and distribution system will help. This could range from a simple spreadsheet model to a sophisticated turnkey application.

An agile manufacturing system, with short cycle times and flexible production capacity, is your best defense against the double-edged sword of stockouts and excessive inventories. Do not underestimate the cost of a stockout. You have gone to a lot of trouble to mount the invasion and attack the niche. Lost credibility from stockouts during a mainstream product launch can be devastating.

Transition: The Crisis of Sustained Expansion. Your company must be prepared to keep delivering whole-product solutions as fast as the market will allow. Sales will ramp up rapidly as the diffusion process takes hold. There will be an inflection, the point at which the unit sales rate peaks and then begins to decline as you begin to approach your equilibrium share of the targeted industry segment. This is about the right time to begin attacking other segments. The strategy for this transition to a multisegment expansion has been in place for a long time and was adjusted just before the product launch. Now it is time to revisit it again in light of current events.

You should reanalyze cash flow at this point. Ideally, you will be able to finance sustained expansion out of earnings, but you may need additional debt or equity financing. Eventually your earnings will be strong enough to pay down long-term debt to a level that brings your financial ratios within ranges desired by investors and industry analysts. This creates evidence of the financial strength your company needs to win its final positioning battle.

The Next Three Organizational Growth Stages

This section describes Stages 2, 3, and 4 of the organizational growth process. Once commitments are made, the business becomes a new venture (Stage 2). Expansion (Stage 3) comes when the organization must grow rapidly to support market creation and product development activities of increasing scope and intensity. The organization enters the fourth stage, professionalization, when it starts paying serious attention to rules, limits, and operating policy.

Organizational Growth Stage 2: New Venture

The new venture starts when the founders commit resources. The legal form of the business is less important than the fact that a sacrifice has been made to launch the enterprise. The meter is now running. The survival task of a new venture is to prove it can sell a product to customers in its targeted niche.

Human Frame. You need a simplified, working framework to come to grips with the aspects of human nature that are important to your company. There are two basic performance metrics: effectiveness and efficiency. There are also two important time frames: near-term and long-term. If you take these four items as the four dimensions of human nature that are relevant to business, you end up with four basic personality traits:[15]

- Near-term effectiveness (Performer or P-type)
- Near-term efficiency (Administrator or A-type)
- Long-term effectiveness (Entrepreneur or E-type)
- Long-term efficiency (Integrator or I-type)

Psychologists have noted the existence of these four personality types when it comes to solving problems. E-types, for example, are very good at thinking up new things to do and finding new ways of looking at the world. P-types prefer to get things done that are already set right in front of them. A-types like to check things that have already been done and set up systems to get them done right. I-types enjoy getting everyone to work together as a team.

A new venture must have a strong dose of P-type personalities, plus smaller doses of A-, E-, and I-types for checking and balancing. The long-term vision has already been defined by a strong dose of E-types during the pre-commitment stage. Near-term survival now hinges on doing, not dreaming. There is not enough mental energy in the new venture to sustain much more over-the-horizon E-type thinking *and* get effective near-term performance. The E-type will have another day in the sun, but not during the new venture stage.

Structural Frame. The new venture is deceptive in its apparent simplicity. It is really just as challenging to manage as a later stage organization. This often catches entrepreneurs off guard. An effective structure does not just happen. It is designed. Figure 12 shows the basic relationships between organizational design variables.

Three major sets of choices establish the structural frame: your choice of business strategy, your choice of organizing mode, and your choice of methods for integrating individuals. Together, the organizational design variables comprise a complete structural framework.

Political Frame. The political frame provides a different view about the origin and intent of corporate goals. In this view the organization is a collection of powerful individuals and interest groups. Each has its own objectives

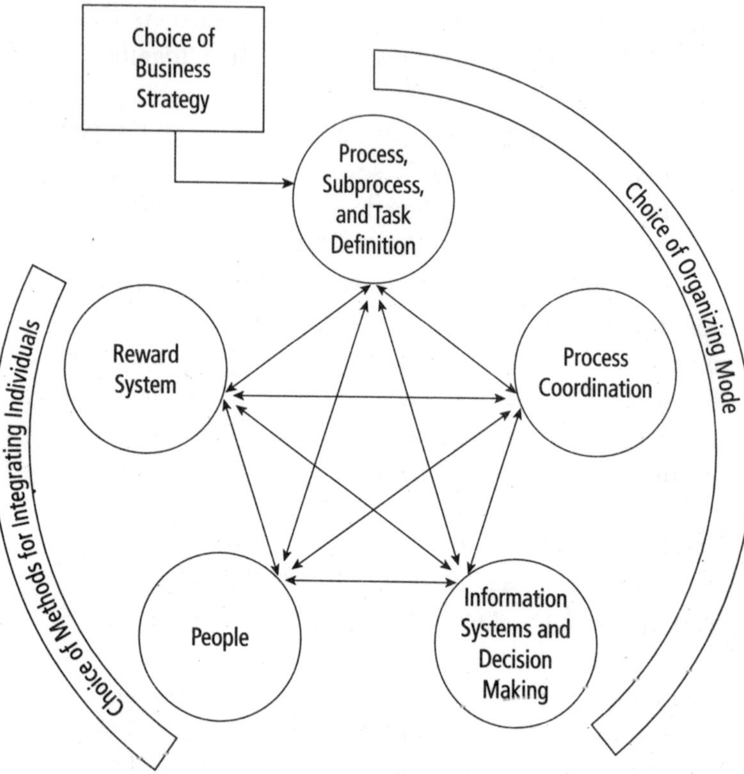

Figure 12. Basic relationships between organizational design variables (adapted from Galbraith[16])

and controls certain resources. These resources are bargaining chips for influencing the goals and actions of other coalitions. The formal management structure shows up in the political frame as just another coalition, with its own resources and goals.

Forget about relying solely on your title and the formal authority that comes with it. When you get into a political firefight, you will need additional means to prevail. Formal authority is an obvious source of political power, but there is also personal power. Charisma, the ability to attract followers, a commanding presence, a way with words and the ability to articulate a vision are all elements of personal power. Unique knowledge or expertise also confers power. Information, know-how, an ability to get important things done, and mastery of unique skills all constitute power. The ability to deliver and withhold rewards is a great source of political power. Examples are the ability to invest money or obtain the backing of investors, the capacity to create or eliminate jobs, or the means to obtain the support of elected officials and the favor of government regulators. Last but not least is coercion, the ability to walk off the job, disrupt operations, or trigger some other unpleasant event unless demands are met.

The more kinds of political power you possess, the less of any one you must exercise. This is important because excessive use of any one kind of political power becomes a visible irritant to those on the receiving end. It breeds resentment and invites retribution. Stay below the threshold and people may not even be aware that these political weapons are being deployed.

Cultural Frame. Corporate culture comes complete with its own symbolism, history, and values. These relate to work ethic, mode of dress, the way customers are treated, and the level of trust between employees and managers. Over time, a combination of written and unwritten rules permeates the company. Behavior in the workplace gravitates toward accepted norms.

Transition: The Crisis of Leadership. The founders of most new ventures are product-oriented risk takers with little or no patience for administration. Founders directly supervise, or do, everything themselves. Administrative systems are minimal. The founder *is* the business. The founder does all the important jobs, supplies most of the energy, and bails out the company when necessary.

The new venture plunges ahead, not knowing or caring about its strengths and weaknesses. The mix of people is skewed toward dreamers and doers, and away from checkers and organizers. The information-handling load reaches, then exceeds, the level the founder can handle. Bad decisions are made. Founders typically underestimate needed cash and working capital. They are perfectly willing to roll the dice in hopes that cash will magically appear when needed. But strong sales growth, even if it occurs, just worsens the cash flow problem. Deals made with friends while trying to build commitment now come back to haunt the founder. Investors get nervous. Infighting begins.

A crisis of leadership occurs. The ensuing revolution may be bloodless or otherwise, but there *will* be a revolution–a change of direction. There must be. The founder must either rise to the challenge or be replaced. The death of the company is the only alternative. Rising to the challenge is much easier said than done. For a founder who is temperamentally unsuited to be a manager, it takes a supreme act of will. The new venture passes the crisis when it gains a strong business manager who is acceptable to the owners and who can pull the organization together. Now the organization is ready for the expansion stage.

Organizational Growth
Stage 3: Expansion

In its expansion stage, the organization must demonstrate its ability to acquire additional resources and build complex operational systems.

Human Frame. The P-types have served the organization well by pulling it through the new venture stage and into the expansion stage. The product is selling in the targeted niche. Cash flow has stabilized. Viability is proven. This frees up enough mental energy to bring the E-types back onto center stage. The right mix of personalities for the expansion stage is: dominant-P *and* dominant-E plus smaller doses of A-types and I-types for checking and balancing. This makes the expansion stage highly *effectiveness*-oriented, and gives it a good balance of near-term and long-term perspectives.

Structural Frame. The answer to the information overload problem lies within the structural frame. You must transfer decision-making authority and responsibility to others. You have an important choice to make between two distinct organizing modes: task-centered or process-centered. I strongly recommend process-centered. Name your core processes. Start with the three prime movers—organizational growth, market creation, and product development. Break them down into subprocesses. Continue until you arrive at individual tasks. Involve your whole team in the exercise. Then give your seconds-in-command ownership of important processes that support the prime movers.

You may decide to set up engineering, marketing and sales, production, and finance and administration departments. Make sure these departments are centers of excellence for the respective knowledge domains, *not* turf-oriented centers of power in their own right. Back up this process-centered division of labor with a reward system that recognizes end-to-end process *results,* not departmental turf or mere functional efforts.

Political Frame. Expect political infighting. For example, the natural tension between the P-types and the E-types that propels the company through its expansion stage can erupt into political conflict. This often arises at the interface between engineering design and manufacturing. The expansion stage company is just as personality-driven as the new venture, but now there are multiple power centers because of its new structure. Rapid growth means there is more to fight about, and the company still lacks the rules and cultural norms that transcend egos and constrain empire building.

Cultural Frame. The expansion stage culture centers around the values of the P-types and E-types that dominate it. The company is highly results-oriented. There are dreamers, and there are those who want those dreams realized right away. The company is therefore impatient, even frantic. It pushes ahead in many directions at once, usually biting off more than it can chew. Controls, limits, and job descriptions are deemed a drag on progress. The organization is built on the fly to fit the whims of strong personalities. Administrators and synergists take a backseat to doers and dreamers. There is frequent talk of the big hit, the home run.

Transition: The Crisis of Autonomy. The managers in charge of key processes flex their muscles and head off in alarming new directions. They decide things differently than the founder would have. When mistakes happen, the founder feels blindsided and threatened. The founder explodes and goes back to reviewing every decision before it is final. Now, however, there is no corporate insulation from the heat generated by the rapidly expanding company. Before long it is back to delegation. Yet the unspoken message is: "Do it my way." The managers in charge try, but they still apply different values and use different logic. With no guidelines in place, the managers cannot use their delegated power effectively without getting crosswise with other parts of the organization. It is only a matter of time until serious crises erupt. Survival now depends on a leader who can pull the rudderless organization up by its bootstraps.

Organizational Growth Stage 4: Professionalization

In its professionalization stage, the organization must develop more formalized management systems and establish guidelines to govern their activities.

Human Frame. There is only so much mental energy to go around, and building a sound administrative system takes a lot of mental energy. Something has to give. Bringing the A-types out onto center stage means that either the P-types or the E-types will have to give ground. Which should it be?

Do not dare cut into the entrepreneurial spirit at this stage. Instead, throttle back temporarily on the P-types. Why? Because if you cut back the E-types now, your organization will be left with *only* a short-term focus. The entrepreneurial types are your ticket to the future.

Structural Frame. The manager of a professionalized business knows the difference between *delegation* and *decentralization.* Delegation means to assign a task and monitor its performance. The instructions that go with a delegated task are specific to that task. Decentralization means turning over the power to initiate decisions about what tasks to perform. In doing so, the central power creates *multiple power centers.* But these dispersed power centers must not be strung out in a vacuum. The space between them and the central authority must be spanned with a policy structure that defines expected performance goals *and* draws clear boundaries around the range of permissible actions. These boundaries are just as important as the goals. They make it clear what markets will *not* be entered, what management practices will *not* be used and what financial constraints will *not* be violated.

Political Frame. The darker side of human nature exploits imperfections in the policy structure. There can be a *civil war.* It usually starts in one of the provinces. The distance created by decentralization breeds parochial attitudes. Advocates and opponents of different projects and systems form cliques. An us-versus-them mentality rears its ugly head. This infighting uses up valuable energy. Beefed-up stock options and profit sharing only draw attention to the fact that there is more to fight about. Partisan demands take on new intensity. Some people may have to be fired.

Cultural Frame. The culture shifts in the direction of the dominant personality types who now hold sway, the E-types and the A-types. Rules and policies are in vogue, together with big-picture thinking and innovation. It is acceptable to spend time talking about how the company should operate internally and what business it should *not* be pursuing.

There is no more snapping back and forth between centralization and decentralization. Communication with your functional managers becomes less frequent. The nature of the communication changes, too. Instead of haggling about the details of internal operations, you meet periodically to review top-level performance, fine-tune objectives, and identify companywide issues. Finger-pointing and turf wars turn into handshakes and win-win alliances. Investors see the company doing what it said it would do. Confidence builds.

Transition: The Crisis of Control. No amount of professional glue can hold human nature in check forever. Some senior managers will want to run their own shows without coordinating with the rest of the organization. You are well beyond the point of no return. You cannot recentralize power. The only viable course is straight ahead. Your company must survive another lifecycle transition.

The new element you must add is better coordination. You may decide to treat each product group as a profit center in its own right, with return on invested capital used as an important criterion for allocating funds. You may need a better system to coordinate central R&D with that done by the business units. Cash management should be centralized for maximum leverage. Capital expenditures should be targeted on long-term objectives that the senior managers all understand. The reward system may need tuning up to buy loyalty and align personal aspirations with corporate success.

IV.

Running the Mature Company

Mature geological forms, according to Webster, have "reached maximum development of topographical form or vigor of action, as with streams that have no plains and that have begun to widen rather than deepen their valleys." The mature company has hit its stride. Its understanding of the prime mover growth processes has reached adequate depth. It has not yet attained its maximum size, but is still vigorously "broadening its valley." Maturity refers to the viability of the growth processes themselves, not the absolute size and scope already attained. Figure 13 shows what happens to the three prime movers–market creation, product development, and organizational growth–as the company reaches maturity. The company can continue to expand indefinitely if its leadership stands vigilant guard against smothered innovation, complacency, and risk aversion. But if these telltale signs become the order of the day, the company will descend into bureaucracy and, ultimately, death.

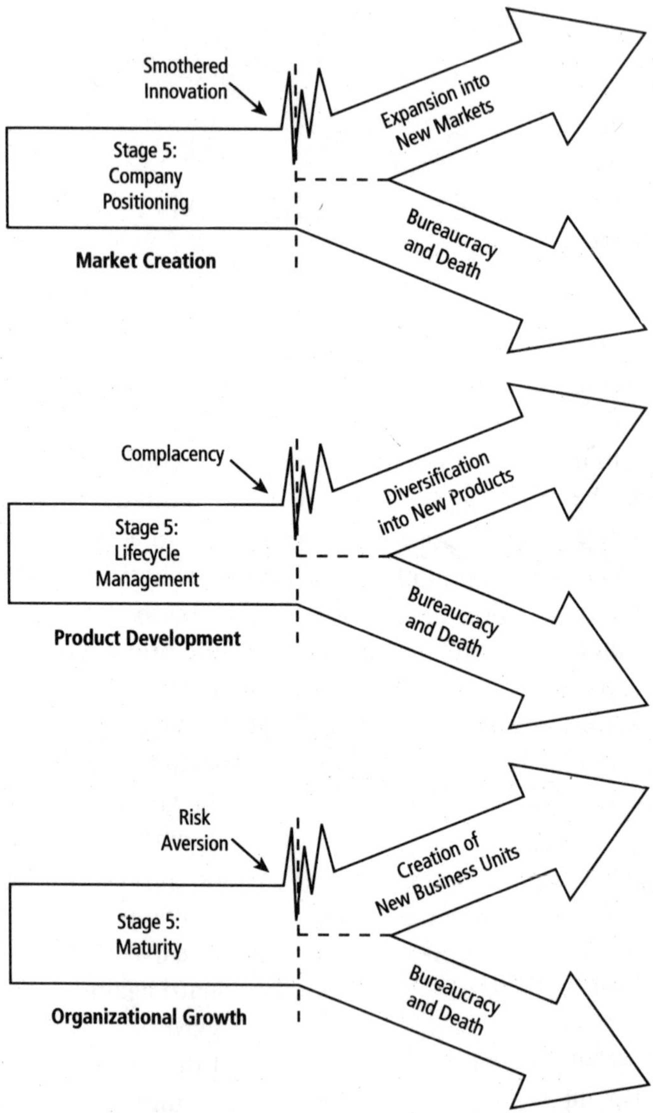

Figure 13. The prime movers as the company reaches maturity

Market Creation Stage 5: Company Positioning

The marketplace already understands how your products stack up against those offered by competitors. It now asks a different question. Can your company itself be valued as a source of equally good and better products long into the future?

Value Chain Frame. Now that you have its attention, the marketplace would like to peer into all aspects of your company's value chain and get a warm feeling about everything you are doing. Since that requires too much work, the marketplace seeks a shortcut answer. It turns to financial stability as the one metric it can understand.

Earnings reports, plant expansions, and major capitalizations translate into financial stability in the eyes of customers. A loss, on the other hand, signals that your company may be about to cut back on product development, lose key talent, and falter in its customer service. Pragmatist customers are loyal. They will hope for the best, but fear the worst.

Diffusion of Innovation Frame. The diffusion process is up and running again. Now, you must repeat the performance in other segments. Let the diffusion process follow the path of least resistance. "Run the table" by executing your industry segmentation strategy. Winning over each new industry segment is a replay of a battle you have already fought and won. You must establish a new whole-product-based total solution within each new segment you attack. Your arsenal now includes references from satisfied pragmatists. The FUD attacks will continue, but your whole-product armor is tougher than ever. Always frame the competition, then kill it with superior performance.

Good corporate positioning provides the muscle to power through the early majority and move on to win over the even more pragmatic late majority. Together, these two groups make up two-thirds of the entire market. The battle to win them over ultimately makes or breaks the company.

Industry Segmentation Frame. The industries you are selling to are dynamic. Anything that changes the rules of the competitive game or the industry's basic structure will also change the way it is segmented. Rethink your segmentation matrix continually. Reassess competitors' positions. Pinpoint segments where they are strong, where they are weak, or where they have abandoned the field. Watch especially for emerging segments that look attractive. Target them and win them over before competitors figure it out.

Continue to look for leverage between segments. I have already talked about leveraging customer relationships and product development efforts by migrating along rows and columns of the segmentation matrix. But there are many other forms of intersegment leverage. For example, you can:

Support multiple segments via the same channel or by using the same logistics

- Cross-sell products among segments
- Share advertising and promotional resources
- Share sales, service, and order processing operations
- Use the same components in multiple products
- Share production or final assembly facilities
- Leverage overhead activities like finance, accounting, and personnel
- Use joint procurement to enhance leverage with your suppliers
- Extend product lines to enhance appeal to late majority and laggard buyers

Marketing Communications Frame. The marketing communications process is now reaching its most mature stage. The company and its customers have each formed mental pictures of each other. The financial health of the company is a central theme. Company positioning and financial viability reinforce one another. Good company positioning makes capital easier to raise. The resulting financial strength enhances the company's positioning. Success breeds success in other ways, too. Everyone wants a relationship with the market leader. Your product development people are approached with many of the best ideas. Attractive acquisition candidates appear. Strategic alliances materialize.

Product Development Stage 5: Lifecycle Management

In the lifecycle management stage, your focus shifts from a single product to multiple products introduced over a longer period of time and to additional product/market segments.

Product Strategy Frame. The long-term goal of product lifecycle management is sustained profitability over time, as shown in Figure 14. Product 1 Profit is negative during introduction, rises rapidly as sales grow, plateaus as the market matures, and declines as the market saturates. Development and market entry costs will eventually be recouped out of earnings. This is the period investors have been looking forward to. It is the time the return on their investment is realized. The lifecycle of the product must be managed throughout its growth, maturity, and decline phases to maximize the return. Your main focus will become the behavior of costs. Keeping bureaucracy in check and innovation alive are critical long-term success factors. Competitive pressure is likely to drive prices down sooner or later. When it does, you should have enough margin built in to price competitively and still earn a profit.

Figure 14 also shows the sales and profit curves for other products superimposed on those for Product 1. Combined sales and profit over many products, shown by the dashed lines in Figure 14, can generate performance that continues to grow over time.

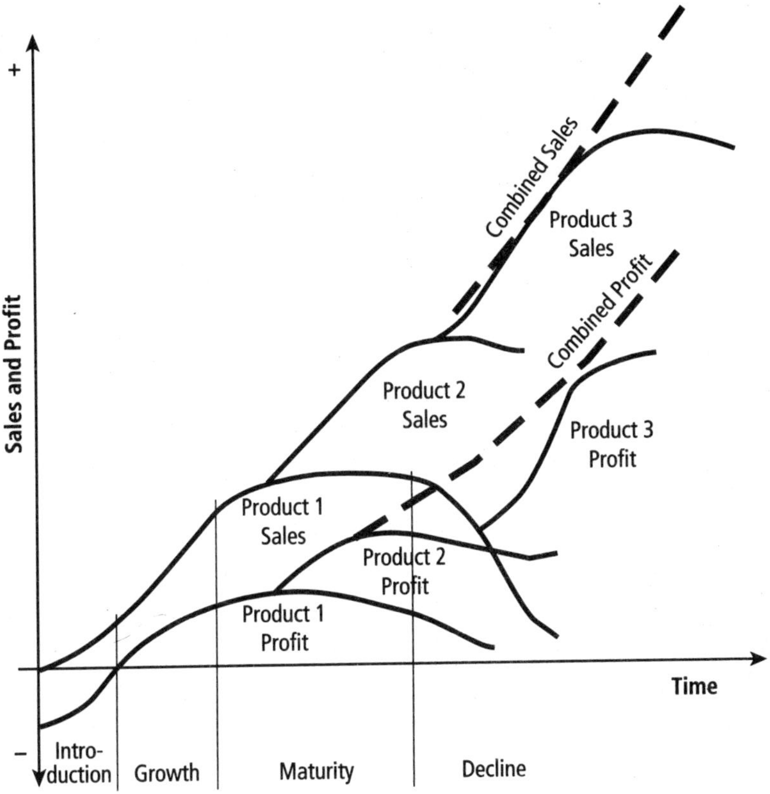

Figure 14. Profitability and sales over the product life cycle

Engineering Design Frame. The engineering designers stay busier than ever supporting new product development efforts and new releases of existing products. The disciplines brought to bear during the lifecycle management stage include specification verification, drawing release, documentation, production readiness, manufacturing procedures, tooling design and release, quality control, configuration management, quality assurance, spares provisioning, environmental stress screening, and sustaining engineering.

Engineering analysis of operational problems enhances earlier solutions. It provides an opportunity to identify problems that might otherwise go unreported. Solutions may include alternative maintenance techniques or design improvements to prolong operating life.

Physical Transformation Frame. The focus of attention in the physical transformation frame shifts to the productive efficiency of the whole enterprise. Long-term viability hinges on the company's ability to organize itself into an efficient system for transforming input resources (materials, components, energy, and information) into value-added products customers are willing to pay for. Overhead support for primary value-added processes must be adequate, but minimal. Process-centered organizations have a much better chance of achieving long-term viability. They keep their activities externally focused. Everything either supports the end-user directly or enables another process that does.

Resource Frame. The resource frame must be monitored to detect the onset of one last transition, the decline and ultimate phase-out of the product. This is not as simple as it may sound. You may be witnessing a classic market saturation phenomenon (a true decline) or just a temporary downturn due to other conditions. It is sometimes possible to redefine the industry segment through technological innovation or strategic maneuvering, so that it becomes no longer saturated. Pulling a product off the market prematurely wastes the profit potential its remaining life would have generated. This would be unfortunate, since development and market entry costs have long since been amortized.

Make every effort to keep mature products ticking away as *money machines*. For example, replacement sales or second sales can change the dynamics of saturation dramatically. This is the basis of the classic razor blade business. The long-term money is in the blades, not the razor. Launching a new generation product will rob sales from the old product. Therefore timing is critical. The resource trade-off deserves careful modeling.

Organizational Growth Stage 5: Maturity

Your main challenge in the maturity stage is to establish and maintain a viable corporate culture that transcends individual personalities. The organization's embedded values and behavioral norms define its identity. They reflect what the company stands for in its products and services, in the management of its people, and in its dealings with customers, suppliers and strategic partners. The view from all four organizational growth frames will help you meet the challenge of operating a mature company.

Human Frame. Once you have passed through the crisis of control, it is time to throttle up the P-types again. It is as if you have installed a new transmission during the professionalization stage. Now it is time to put the pedal to the metal again! The power generated by your revenue engine can now make it all the way to the profit wheels without stripping any gears.

The mental energy devoted to professionalizing the company can now be directed back to performance. For the first time, your organization can meet the demands of *three* dominant personality types at the same time: P-types (Performers), A-types (Administrators), and E-types (Entrepreneurs). Of course, you still need a smaller dose of I-types for checking and balancing. The horse is now before the cart. The organization drives its opportunities, rather than being driven by them. It knows what not to pursue just as well as it knows what to go after with all its might.

Structural Frame. Strategic planning is a flexible, continuous process, but commitments are made only after intensive review to balance risks and rewards. Hiring and promotion are well regulated. The reward system incorporates stock options and profit sharing tied to the health of the business as a whole. The executives in charge of decentralized business units have broad authority to operate within a framework they helped establish. You demand results, but do not blame people who take calculated risks and fail.

Your production is high-volume. Your markets are international. Your key concerns are how to finance more growth. Improved access to long-term credit further leverages your investors' capital. New business ideas that demonstrate technical feasibility and survive market testing receive the capital they need to fuel internal growth.

You periodically screen other companies as acquisition candidates.

Political Frame. The leader of a mature company spends a lot of time reminding people about the common purpose that pulls everything together. The leader strives to stake out a "share" of everyone's mind that is dedicated to the company's mission and objectives. Maturity, however, is not utopia. The company is still staffed with humans, and humans, as Aristotle put it, are "political animal[s]." The well-balanced organizational structure still sits atop a jungle, alive and screaming with the self-interests, virtues, and vices of complex individuals. You have learned not to ignore politics. Instead, you take it in stride.

The political arena has its own rules. The business, with all its strategies, structures, and operating policies, occupies only part of peoples' overall *share of mind.* Sharp contrasts abound in values, beliefs, emotions, backgrounds, worldviews, and basic working assumptions about life. These uncharted regions lie beneath the organization's "cerebral cortex." Yet they surface instantly when triggered by resource allocation decisions or shifts in the power structure. Coalitions form to advance positions that appear rational on the surface, but are really rooted in subjective political turf.

Cultural Frame. The culture of a mature company perpetuates itself apart from founders and superstar personalities. Your top executives have assumed responsibility for establishing and maintaining formal systems. These keep things running smoothly most of the time. Some functions, such as cash management and employee benefits, are centralized to get maximum leverage. Lateral groups cut across the decentralized business units, bringing the power of the whole corporation to bear on focused market niches. Teams form in direct response to problems or opportunities spotted by people close to the action. These transcend organization charts and job descriptions. Some get formalized as task forces or new product groups. Many come and go as informal parts of the "adhocracy."

Forestalling Death by Bureaucracy

You have a good thing going as leader of a mature company. Your job now is to keep it going. The final set of life-cycle transitions, shown in Figure 13 (page 74), are to be *avoided,* not traversed. Until this point in the life of your company you have always strived to achieve the next growth stage. This changes at maturity. You must strive now to *prevent* nature from taking its course, because that course leads to bureaucracy and death. To succeed, you have to address these three challenges:

- The Crisis of Smothered Innovation. You must find ways to build innovation into the fabric of your organization. Set up policies and operating procedures that create a business environment conducive to innovation. The company's policies and reward systems should make the bird in the bush just as attractive to managers as the bird in the hand.
- The Crisis of Complacency. Complacency invites defeat at the hands of aggressive competitors. If

things seem quiet in the marketplace, your product development team should attack itself. It must continue to challenge assumptions. It should strive to beat its own track record, which becomes more difficult with each success. Ultimate viability of the product development process is a matter of corporate culture, just as it is in the case of market creation and organizational growth.

The Crisis of Risk Aversion. Running a mature company is like balancing a broom on the palm of your hand. Risk aversion pulls the company one way. Risk taking pulls it the other. How do you run the company in a controlled, predictable manner and still keep innovation alive? It isn't easy. You have to work at it. The key is to realize that innovation cannot coexist with daily operations. The crisis of the day *always* preempts resources needed for innovation. Embryonic ideas get trampled to death by the thundering herd of daily business problems. Yet the herd itself will eventually go extinct if new business ideas are not conceived, nurtured, and allowed to mature.

V.

Supporting Disciplines

It is important to distinguish between the prime mover processes and the supporting disciplines. The prime mover processes have a life of their own. The supporting disciplines are relatively static. The prime mover processes have growth stages. The supporting disciplines do not. If you do not keep these distinctions in mind, you may start treating supporting disciplines as if they were prime movers. Overemphasizing competitive strategy, for example, can lead you to fixate on product features. The "world-will-beat-a-path-to-my-door" syndrome stems from a false hope that some unique distinguishing feature of a new product is all you need to build a business. Many entrepreneurs believe adequate financing is all they need to succeed. To say, "just provide the cash I need and the rest will happen," is a sure sign that the cart is before the horse. Business law, and the many regulations you must follow, can also drive you to distraction, literally. Getting caught up in legal concerns and administrative details can distract you from your main job as owner of the three prime mover processes. Lawyers are necessary to keep you from running aground, but never let your lawyer drive the boat.

Competitive Strategy: The Rules of Engagement

Competitive strategy begins with an understanding of the fundamental factors that determine the nature of competition. There are basically just three competitive strategies: differentiation, cost leadership, and focus. Focus can be combined with either differentiation or cost leadership to form a hybrid strategy. However, it is generally not wise to combine differentiation and cost leadership unless you really know what you are doing. These two fundamentally different kinds of strategy usually require different financial structures, different types of key people, and different corporate cultures.

The key elements of competitive strategy that affect your business-building efforts include market signals, industry structure, building competitive advantage, the value chain, industry segmentation, and competitor intelligence.[17]

Finance: Lifeblood of the Enterprise

Financial resources can be brought into your company from external sources of finance, by retained earnings from operations, and through acquisitions or mergers. Finance links the need to fund your company with the needs of investors to realize a return on their capital. If you are attempting to raise funds externally, you must know the sources most and least likely to provide financing in your situation. Your goal is to raise funds efficiently and at reasonable cost.

You need a working knowledge of the following financial topics: assets, external sources of finance, internal sources of finance, sustainable growth, debt and equity, financial ratios, cost of debt, cost of equity, raising equity capital, equity and debt instruments, sources of capital, and start-up financing.

Business Law: Standing Your Ground

"Where-ever the Law ends," wrote John Locke in *The Second Treatise on Government* in 1690, "tyranny begins." The law is the ground on which you stand when you build your business. Without it, you could not raise capital, extend credit, make a contract, or protect your intellectual property without also raising your own private army to enforce these agreements. The flip side is that the law restrains your own actions. So far, so good. Real problems arise, however, from contradictory laws, predatory manipulation of the law, and the sheer complexity of it all. It was such perversions of the law that inspired William Shakespeare to write in 1591, "The first thing we'll do, let's kill all the lawyers." (*Henry VI,* Part II)

The areas of the law that concern you in business include: court systems and lawsuits, crimes and torts, contracts, commercial paper, banking, agency, corporations and other forms of business organization, property (including intellectual property), creditor's rights and protection of debtors, and regulatory law.

VI.

Required Skills

Many skills are required to run a business. First-time entrepreneurs are often unfamiliar with most of them, which leads to a sense of foreboding. However, as previously discussed, all you need to pay attention to when steering the company ship are three prime movers–organizational growth, market creation, and product development–and the three supporting disciplines–competitive strategy, finance, and business law. Your sailors, however, will need to have the skills summarized in Figure 15 to keep the rigging intact.

The need to access one or more of these skills is triggered by both the prime mover processes and the supporting disciplines. Developing a skills inventory checklist for yourself and your team will help you pinpoint the weak spots. Remember, these skills are for sale. Do not be intimidated if you do not have the one you need. Go out and get it.

- ❒ Accounting
- ❒ Accounting Controls
- ❒ Administrative Skills
- ❒ Assertiveness
- ❒ Communication Skills
- ❒ Computer Network Management
- ❒ Corporate Governance
- ❒ Crisis Planning and Disaster Recovery
- ❒ Customer Service
- ❒ Dealing with Lawyers
- ❒ Distribution Management
- ❒ Engineering Design
- ❒ Environmental Risk Management
- ❒ Facilities Management
- ❒ Financial Management
- ❒ Group Discussion Leadership
- ❒ Human Resources Management
- ❒ Information Systems Deployment
- ❒ Insurance and Risk Management
- ❒ Intellectual Property Management
- ❒ International Relations
- ❒ Internet Access and Use
- ❒ Inventory Management
- ❒ Investor Relations
- ❒ Languages
- ❒ Management Skills
- ❒ Manufacturing Resources Planning
- ❒ Manufacturing System Layout
- ❒ Marketing Management
- ❒ Leadership Skills
- ❒ Motivation and Image-Building
- ❒ Multimedia Techniques
- ❒ Negotiating Skills
- ❒ Office Management
- ❒ Operational Planning
- ❒ Organizational Skills
- ❒ Procurement and Supplier Management
- ❒ Productive Meetings
- ❒ Project Management
- ❒ Quality Control Methods
- ❒ Research and Development Management
- ❒ Sales Force Management
- ❒ Selling
- ❒ Shop Foor Execution and Control
- ❒ Strategic Planning
- ❒ Taxes
- ❒ Team Building
- ❒ Training
- ❒ Treasury Management
- ❒ Valuation of Companies

Figure 15. Categories of required skills

The Skills You Should Master Yourself

There are two situations in which you should master certain skills yourself, instead of delegating the work to others: when you are just starting the business and have no way to buy or otherwise access the required skill (for example, keeping the books or designing the first feasibility demonstration); and when the skill is one you will need personally over the long haul to sustain the organization (such as leadership or communication).

Do not feel that lack of in-depth professional training in one or more important business skills is a serious handicap. Amateur working knowledge of professional disciplines like accounting and law is adequate to run the business. The key is to be sensitive to your limitations. You need to know when you are getting in over your head and then seek professional help. When you do hire professionals, listen attentively to every word they say as they apply their knowledge to your problems. Ask questions. Learn. Fill in the cracks. Let them get on with their jobs, but use the opportunity to build your own working knowledge about their respective disciplines.

The working knowledge you are looking for is not so much the technical details, but how their profession works. People enjoy talking about their professions. Asking these questions builds your own working knowledge and your relationship with these people at the same time.

The Skills Your Team Must Have

The skills your team should have are the ones that support the strategic architecture of your company. What is strategic architecture? Start with your customers. Specifically, note the industry segments you are targeting or already doing business with and the respective core benefits propositions delivered to customers in those segments. The same core benefits propositions that drive market creation and product development also drive your strategic architecture.

You must establish certain core competencies within the organization to deliver the core benefits propositions to which you have committed the company. Core competencies are domains of expertise or capability. Software development is an example of a core competency. Electromechanical design is another. Financial management, investor relations, marketing, sales, promotion, procurement, distribution, shop floor layout, and production system design are other examples. Multiple core competencies are usually needed to deliver a given core benefit proposition. Write this mapping down for your own business. It's important to understand it explicitly.

The required skills are the ones that support the core competencies you have identified. Each core competency is based on a particular body of knowledge. Examine this body of knowledge. Ask questions of your own people and other experts. Use what you find out to list skills required to support each core competency. That is the list your team, as a whole, must have.

The Skills You Should Buy Only When You Need Them

If your plan calls for temporary, exploratory work that depends on a certain discipline, or if you just cannot afford to staff up for it right now, then outsource it. You can always change your mind later and bring the skill in-house if you decide it really supports a core competency. Staffing up commits your company to employee benefits, and your employees to family and career goals that you may have to disrupt later. Be very careful about staffing up to support what looks like a core competency but isn't.

Building Your Skills Inventory

It is good to keep track of who has what skills as your company grows. Start with the list of skills you built for the strategic architecture exercise. This will give people an example of what you are talking about. Just ask them to check off any skills on the list they already have, and even note skills they would like to develop.

VII.

Lifecycle Navigation in the Real World

LET'S EXPLORE LIFECYCLE NAVIGATION as it applies in the real world, starting with absolute situation awareness. I suggest you develop an absolute situation awareness checklist based on the reframing technique. This will resemble the list a warship captain would check periodically in normal operations and with more intensity in the heat of battle. The warship captain's framework comes from military training and is perfected with experience. Yours comes from the lifecycle navigation framework. It, too, will be perfected based on your own experience.

The most important reason for systematic reframing is to avoid being blindsided by an impending lifecycle transition. It's like sweeping the sky with radar beams, deploying undersea listening devices, and reviewing satellite reconnaissance photographs. If there is trouble brewing or opportunity knocking, it may show up in any one of these intelligence-gathering frames. But you never know which one ahead of time, so you have to continually scan them all.

Lessons from Experience

In real organizations, the prime movers can stall, fall back, and restart. Sometimes the growth stage transitions happen spontaneously. At other times you must actively lead the organization from one stage to the next. In any case, you dare not let a growth stage transition take you by surprise. There are different rules for operating within each stage. Each has its own special character. Can you skip a stage? Only in rare circumstances. The reason is that the previous stage sets up preconditions for the next. Skipping a stage introduces instabilities from which an organization seldom recovers.

The prime mover processes can get out of alignment. One or more may stagnate. They usually run afoul of constraints imposed by the supporting disciplines when these things happen. The framework needs constant attention to keep it in good working order. Lack of diligence blocks the views from one or more of the twelve frames, inviting unwelcome surprises.

Experience shows, too, that the range of possible growth scenarios is much richer than you might imagine. One, to be sure, is steady, well-aligned growth through the five stages of each prime mover. The industry you compete in may dictate that the business either grows or dies. Most high-technology industries are this way. But a service business in a slowly growing community or a franchise business with a limited territory could let you safely disengage once viability is proven. Events may force the company to fold and liquidate its assets. Sometimes a company can be restarted by dropping its prime movers back to an earlier stage and rebuilding them. If so, the framework can be used to bring the prime movers back into alignment, salvage the pieces, and get the enterprise back into fighting trim again.

Each transitional crisis requires leadership to bring the company through unscathed. Any one of these crises could sink the ship. You should take each one seriously. Put a plan in place to navigate through it and execute the plan. Often, you will be handling two or more lifecycle transitions at the same time. Leadership is:

1. reparing the organization for the next growth stage of each prime mover process
2. aligning the personal goals and aspirations of employees with the strategic intent of the organization

Management is:

1. navigating the organization through the growth stage of each prime mover process
2. aligning actions of employees with the performance requirements of processes needed to implement the chosen strategy

There are many business plan templates and complete examples on how to write a business plan. You will have no trouble at all finding a useful example. Terrance McGarty's *Business Plans That Win Venture Capital*[18] is my personal favorite because it provides sound rationale and computational models along with a good template. Start by writing out your own lifecycle navigation story. Then select the ideas you need to build your business plan around a good template. This way the business plan virtually writes itself.

Taking the Leap

I hope *New Entrepreneur's Guidebook* helps you decide whether entrepreneuring is really for you. If you're ready to go the distance, then take the leap–and take this guidebook with you. Share it with your team. The lifecycle navigation framework provides a common language to describe the life of your company. Celebrate progress as you march through the growth stages. Name the transitions and power through them with confidence. Gain a working knowledge of the supporting disciplines. Pick up required skills as you go. Use the ideas you've mastered to project yourself into the future, bringing conclusions to bear on decisions you must make in the present.

Figure 16 portrays the lifecycle navigation framework ready and waiting to guide you on your way. Godspeed as you set out to build your business!

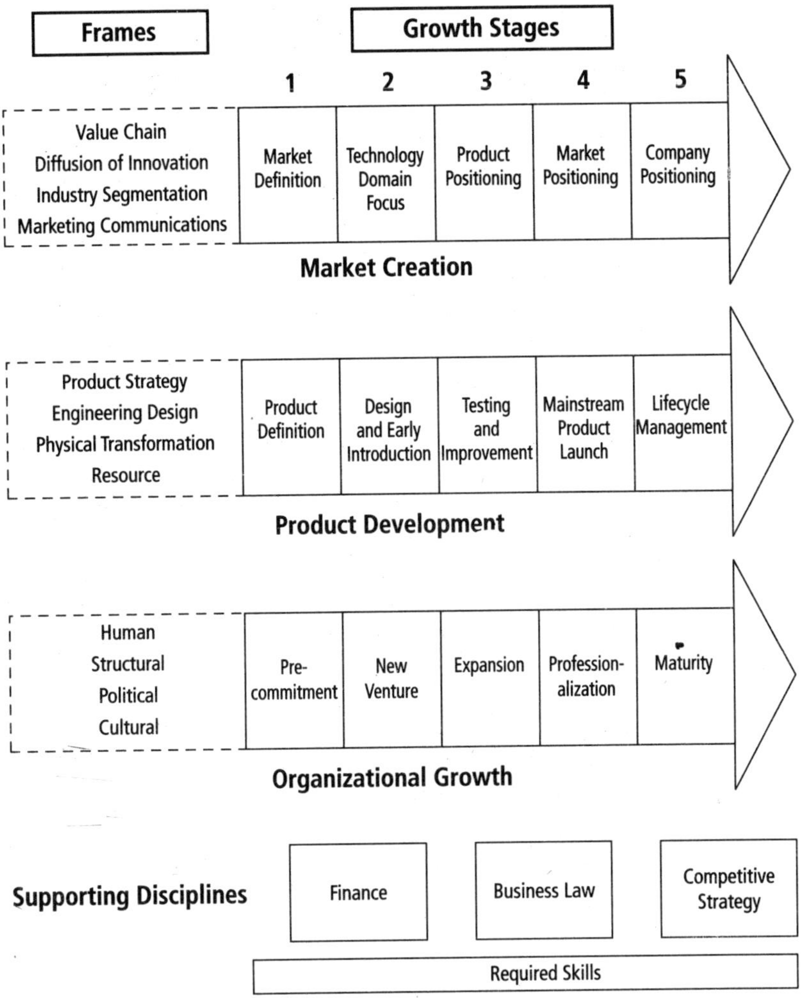

Figure 16. The lifecycle navigation framework

References

1. Hebrews 11:1.
2. Porter, Michael. *Competitive Advantage*. New York: The Free Press, 1985, p. 37.
3. McGarty, Terrance. *Business Plans That Win Venture Capital*. New York: John Wiley & Sons, 1989, p. 62.
4. Rogers, Everett. *Diffusion of Innovations*. New York: The Free Press, 1962, p. 162.
5. Kotler, Philip. *Marketing Management*. Englewood Cliffs, N. J.: Prentice Hall, Sixth Edition, 1988, pp. 261–264.
6. Porter, Michael, op. cit., pp. 233–255.
7. Urban, Glen and John Hauser. *Design and Marketing of New Products*. Englewood Cliffs, N. J.: Prentice Hall, Second Edition, 1993, pp. 19–23.
8. Moore, Geoffrey. *Crossing the Chasm*. New York: Harper Business, 1991, pp. 17–25.
9. Urban, Glen and John Hauser, op. cit., pp. 164–166.
10. Urban, Glen and John Hauser, op. cit., pp. 346–348.
11. Urban, Glen and John Hauser, op. cit., pp. 425–426.
12. Luehrman, Timothy A. "What's It Worth? A General Manager's Guide to Valuation," in *Harvard Business Review*, May–June 1997, p. 133.

13. Luehrman, Timothy A., op. cit., p. 136.

14. Luehrman, Timothy A., op. cit., p. 139.

15. Adizes, Ichak. *Corporate Lifecycles*. Englewood Cliffs, N. J.: Prentice Hall, 1988, pp. 117–127.

16. Galbraith, Jay. *Organizational Design*. Reading, Mass.: Addison-Wesley Publishing Company, 1977, p. 31.

17. Porter, Michael. *Competitive Strategy*. New York: The Free Press, 1980.

18. McGarty, Terrance, op. cit., pp. 326–358.

Further Reading

Drucker, Peter F. *Management: Tasks, Responsibilities, Practices.* New York: Harper Business, 1993.

Flamholtz, Eric G. *Growing Pains, How to Make the Transition from an Entrepreneurship to a Professionally Managed Firm.* San Francisco: Jossey-Bass Publishers, 1991.

Merrill, Ronald E., and Henry D. Sedgwick. *The New Venture Handbook.* New York: AMACOM, 1993.

Moye, John E. *The Law of Business Organizations.* St. Paul, Minnesota: West Publishing Company, Third Edition, 1989.

Rao, Dileep. *Handbook of Business Finance and Capital Sources.* Minneapolis, Minnesota: InterFinance Corporation, a Division of AMACOM, Second Edition, 1982.

Thomas, Robert J. *New Product Development.* New York: John Wiley & Sons, 1983.

About the Author

Paul F. McClure, Ph.D., is president and CEO of Austin, Texas-based Paradigm Corporation, a strategic business development consulting firm that provides executive management, new business development, marketing, and business planning assistance to emerging growth companies and large companies in transition. Dr. McClure has represented venture capital and other investors with due diligence and management services. He specializes in development of industrial technologies, commercialization of university-based inventions, and adaptation of defense-related technologies to private-sector applications.

Dr. McClure is the founder of DTM Corporation, a rapid prototyping company based on technology licensed from the University of Texas at Austin. Founded in 1987, the company was later acquired by a Fortune 500 firm and now does business worldwide. Previously, he worked as a program manager in the defense industry and administered an endowment program for the College of Engineering at UT Austin.

Dr. McClure serves on the National Science Foundation's Advisory Committee for the Small Business Innovation Research Program and speaks regularly at conferences on management and technology commercialization. He is a registered professional engineer in Texas and received his Ph.D. in mechanical engineering from Colorado State University in 1972. He can be reached at the Paradigm Corporation, 7505 Greenhaven Drive, Austin, TX 78757.